REVIEWS

The title says it all really. Christian strongly encourages teachers to teach with passion to promote excellence and love of learning. Teaching is not a job – it is a vocation – and, as he so clearly says, teachers can change lives.

This book is full of inspiration, but also many practical tips and is written by one of the best practitioners I have ever met. Strongly recommend it.

Dame Sally Coates
Executive Principal, Holland Park School

Teach Like Your Heart Is On Fire is a highly recommended and refreshingly beautifully written piece about the central role great teachers play in firing both the hearts and minds of the next generation. As Christian rightly points out, 'your credibility to lead learning is that you yourself continue to be a learner'. This book provides a rich set of ideas around the key themes of character, capacity and culture, which are very important in fostering an environment of growth for all staff. If you are a school leader or teacher looking for a stimulating book about why teaching is a great profession, then this book provides exactly what you need.

Dr Jeffery Quaye OBE
Director of Education and Quality, Aspirations Academies Trust

I loved this book. It had me at the title but then proved to be a brilliant, punchy read. Christian writes with the authentic voice of a long-serving committed pro teacher and leader, bringing together all his experience to convey a wonderful passion for teaching as a craft, fuelled by a desire for excellence. It's hugely informative as well as inspiring and useful as a reflective tool for anyone making their way through their career. Each chapter invites you to 'spark something' – and that 'on fire' energy permeates the whole book. Amongst all the books on classroom techniques, it's refreshing to read a book that's such a powerful celebration of teaching, grounded in realities but reminding us we are 'part of something great'. Bravo!

Tom Sherrington
Director of Teaching WalkThrus

Having known Christian for over ten years, I read this book with eager anticipation and was not disappointed. His passion, enthusiasm, and deep understanding of how schools bring out the best in pupils jumps from every page. If you are looking for a read that relights your passion for the profession or you just want to learn some great new stuff about teaching and leadership, then this is the book for you!

Andy Buck
Author of Leadership Matters and the BASIC book series

Teach Like Your Heart is on Fire is a timely reminder of what sits at the heart of great teaching: *purpose, mindset and craft.* At a moment when workload pressures and wellbeing challenges weigh heavily on the education workforce, this book reconnects teachers with their 'why', blending research, evidence, and practical ideas with the deeply human endeavour of teaching. It champions trust, professional agency and both self and collective efficacy as the foundations on which teachers grow, as individuals and as a profession. Above all, it reminds us of a simple truth: **nobody comes to work to do a bad job**. The final chapter reminds us that when teachers are trusted, supported, and inspired, they flourish, and so do the pupils and communities they serve.

Kathryn Morgan
ASCL Leadership & Workforce Specialist

I am passionate that schools need to be great places to work in order to be great places to learn and the focus of this work often falls on the shoulders of the senior leadership team. Christian's book is a timely reminder that **everyone** in a school shapes the culture and every teacher can make a huge difference every day. I love his simple 3Cs model, which is so simple yet really encapsulates the art of being the very best you can be in the classroom. The book is packed with wonderful stories and anecdotes and I can imagine any teacher, whatever stage of their career, will get so much from the content. A wonderful reminder from a credible teacher and leader of the importance of the heart in teaching and a reminder of the 'why' educators do what they do.

Mandy Coalter
Founder of Talent Architects

ACKNOWLEDGEMENTS

This book has been shaped by many people across different seasons of my professional life, and it reflects their influence more than they may realise.

My thanks to the team at John Catt and subsequently Hachette, whose guidance and contributions made this book possible. Tom Sherrington, Alex Sharratt, Jonathan Barnes, Anders Ingram, Debbie Allen and Emilie Kerton helped turn an idea into a finished work and bring it to readers.

Thank you to the many colleagues at *The Bish*, who played a key role in my growth. Mary Brock, Lorraine Keenan, Keely Cotton, Rhiannon Dillon, John Humber and Angela Laventure created an environment where I could take responsibility, learn quickly and earn my stripes.

I am grateful to the leaders who took chances on me before there was much evidence to justify it. Gillian Warde, Lisa Fenaroli, Phil Wheatley, Jane Lawner, Kirsten Taylor, Sue Jones, Lorraine Taylor and Dino Di Salvo extended trust and opportunity at pivotal moments. Their belief shaped both my development and my understanding of leadership.

I have learned from leaders whose example continues to set a standard for me. Paul Brightly-Jones, Paul Mundy-Castle, Tyrone Myton, Phil Henton, Richard Shaw, Sean Cowley, Dame Sally Coates, Yassamin Sheel MBE, Oli Tomlinson, Leon Wilson, James Eldon and Claire Ferens each demonstrated what principled leadership can look like in practice.

I remain grateful to those who knew me before I became a teacher and spoke to my potential early: Ann Jager, Ian Newman, Dr Karen Lipsedge, Pastor Sam Onyenuforo, Georgina Watson and Aunty Chibs.

Special thanks to Dr Christine Edwards-Leis and Wendy Garrard, whose challenge and encouragement strengthened my confidence and clarity.

Finally, I owe more than I can express to my wife, my children and my wider family and friends. Your love, patience and constancy give meaning to my work and perspective to my ambitions. You are my good and perfect gifts from the Father of Lights, and you make life not only worthwhile, but joyful.

CONTENTS

CONTENTS

INTRODUCTION

Excellence is habit

To be excellent at any craft requires a number of active ingredients, including effort, commitment and tenacity, but I also believe it requires the desire to be excellent. As Aristotle wrote, 'We are what we repeatedly do. Excellence, then, is not an act, but a habit' (Durant, 1926). For somebody to reject average and seek to be the best in their field, they will naturally stand out from their peers. In workplaces everywhere, there are people content with being average; not because they lack the capacity to be more, but because they have been enchanted by the siren song of mediocrity.

In his book *Die Empty*, Todd Henry (2013) writes:

> early in our career ... we at first feel stretched by the new tasks in front of us, but we gradually adapt to expectations and develop the capacity to deal with them. This growth cycle is rapid and steep in our career, when we are constantly facing unfamiliar challenges and in need of developing new skills to deal with them. However, as we progress in our career and accumulate more knowledge, there are fewer experiences that instinctively spark our curiosity and challenge us to rise to the occasion. We quickly grow stagnant, relying on our existing skills to perform our work. These skills may be sufficient, and, depending on how innately talented we are, may even earn us a great amount of respect in our industry, but deep down we know that we're not doing our best work. We know that we're coasting. We've succumbed to mediocrity.

There may be some jobs where being mediocre is OK. Perhaps it isn't that big a deal that my barista was not exceptional at serving me my flat white. Maybe it doesn't matter that the bus driver provided a standard service. There are clearly some jobs where excellence matters (I think it matters everywhere, but that's a different conversation). You would sincerely hope that your surgeon did not slack off in her studies before she performs surgery on you. You would probably pray that your pilot is proficient in navigating planes safely to their destination.

There are some professions where excellence is paramount: I believe teaching is one of them. While we might not be charged with saving lives like a surgeon or preserving lives like a pilot, teachers certainly shape lives.

Everybody should be able to recall a teacher who left an indelible mark on their life, perhaps because of how they made a subject come alive or their example as a role model or their passion and thirst for learning. The more, the merrier. Every young person should encounter an exceptional teacher in their life. Great teachers change lives. And yet, I know there are schools where teachers fall short of being great – not necessarily because they lack the ability, but perhaps because they have adopted attitudes that accept mediocrity.

As Hargreaves and Fullan (2012) write, 'nobody seriously argues that we should fill our schools with low-quality, unmotivated teachers who don't like children, don't know their material, and can't get it across'. On the contrary, we want teachers who desire to be excellent at what they do. What teachers *do* is shape lives, positively or negatively, whether they accept it or not. More than ever, the young people and communities we serve need teachers who ignite the best in themselves and others; those who are determined to be great.

Why I am writing now

In 2019, Grammy award winning rapper J. Cole released the song 'Middle Child'. He raps about being between two generations, like being a big brother and little brother at the same time. That resonated with me.

For me, it describes how I see myself as a teacher and school leader, between two generations: two very distinct eras of education. I feel like a little brother and big brother at the same time. Some of the colleagues who trained, coached and mentored me as a new teacher have retired or are nearing retirement age. At the same time, I am working and leading a new generation of teachers who seek me out for advice, looking to me as a professional role model and example. On the one hand, I have much more room to grow as a teacher and leader, yet on the other I have earned enough experience and expertise to share with others: expertise and experience I have gleaned from others.

I have worked with some amazing people throughout my career – people who have mentored me, coached me, encouraged me, motivated me – but one person who stands out as a colleague is Georgina Watson (née Stevenson). She was a lead practitioner / second-in-department when I joined my first school as a cover supervisor, fresh out of university. She saw my potential – potential I didn't see – and took me under her wing. She bought me a book called *Teach Like Your Hair's on Fire* by Rafe Esquith (2007).

It's the first piece of literature about teaching that I ever read. It details the experiences of Esquith, a classroom teacher teaching fifth-graders (Year 6) in a Los Angeles neighbourhood plagued by poverty and violence. And yet, he managed to teach the unabridged works of Shakespeare to children living in poverty and with English as an additional language.

Before qualifying as a teacher was a twinkle in my eye, that book inspired me and left an indelible mark on my beliefs about what teaching has the power to do. The title of this book pays homage to the book that inspired me.

Perhaps there's somebody out in the world reading this book who would benefit from somebody coming alongside them, putting their arm around them and encouraging them, like Georgina Watson did for me. Well, this is me paying that act of kindness forward. Schön (1995) argues 'reflection-in-action occurs in the medium of words' and so, at the midway point of my career, this book is that medium.

While much has changed in English education, and continues to do so, the principles that underpin what schools do hasn't. Fullan (2003) argues that:

> ... the quality of the public education system relates directly to the quality of life that people enjoy (whether as parents, employers, or citizens), with a strong public education system as the cornerstone of a civil, prosperous, and democratic society.

Teachers build lives. Schools shape society. At least, they should. I strongly believe this. I have seen this happen firsthand, both personally and professionally. My schooling changed the trajectory of my life. I have seen how education has done the same for the lives of thousands of students across my career to date. The impact that a good education can have on a life is unfathomable, and I have found the greatest advocates of this maxim are often those who have lived experiences of the transformative effect of learning.

Lingard et al. (2003) argue that education can 'build upon' and 'reconstitute the habitus', so that those who have been 'socially mobile through education take on a new habitus ... they become the embodiment of the professional positions they take on'. J. Cole wrote 'Middle Child' because he recognised he was at a key juncture in his career and sought to capture his observations about the music industry, namely the hip-hop scene. In a similar way, in this book, I hope to capture my observations about education and how teachers and educational leaders can ensure that schools continue to shape the lives of young people.

How to read this book

Cover to cover

It is totally up to you how you read this book. You can read it from cover to cover, working through the contours of what I believe make a great teacher in the order I have written them. It is my belief that there are three key factors that influence the ability of schools and the teachers who fill them to improve the outcomes of their students:

- Character

- Capacity

- Culture.

These three Cs serve as the sections of this book. Firstly, we have **character**, which focuses on the personal qualities that make up the character of the adults we place in front of our children and young people. The second section addresses the **capacity** of teachers and leaders to continue to develop, grow and adapt to the changing demands of education. Finally, the third section on **culture** explores how teachers and leaders can shape the type of working environments that successfully facilitate the first two sections.

Jump straight in

You could, however, jump to a chapter that resonates with you. I am conscious that, if you are reading this book, you may be looking for some inspiration, so feel free to make a beeline for what you think will serve you best. At the close of each chapter, there is a summary and an activity that I hope will spark something in you. I have tried to provide a practical takeaway for each chapter that you can apply immediately.

Teaching can be a really tough gig. At the time of writing, I have worked in education for almost two decades, and I think it has got harder. In my mind, it is still the best job in the world, but there are so many aspects inside and outside the classroom that can douse the flames of enthusiasm and motivation necessary to facilitate a long career in education. My hope is that what is written here will be an encouragement to you, wherever you are in your career; however you feel about the job; whoever you are. My sincere desire is that, having read this short book, something will spark in you and you will go and *teach like your heart is on fire.*

PART 1
CHARACTER

PART I

CHAPTER 1
START WITH WHY

Great teachers know their origin story

Peter Parker's origin story

Peter Parker failed. When he is bitten by a radioactive spider, instead of selflessly devoting his new superpowers to fighting crime or improving the human condition, Spider-Man uses his gift to establish himself as a television star. After his first performance, he has the opportunity to stop a thief, but fails to do so and allows the criminal to escape. Subsequently, his Uncle Ben is murdered by a burglar – who turns out to be the exact same criminal he failed to apprehend. Grief-stricken, his realisation that *with great power comes great responsibility* shifts his venal motivations towards the altruistic task of serving his local community as a friendly neighbourhood spiderman.

The development of the arachnid superhero is instructive: everybody has an origin story, and these narratives are often a combination of both positive and negative influences. Peter Parker is endowed with superhuman strength and agility. (Yay!) It takes the avoidable loss of his paternal figure to understand how he might use those powers productively. (Boo!) Just as the exposition of the superhero narrative reveals seeds of who the protagonist may become, the lives lived before teaching bear some influence as we develop as education professionals: this is your origin story.

My origin story

I wasn't really able to articulate mine until I had been teaching for several years and completed a master's degree in Educational Leadership. One of my first assignments was to complete a pen portrait, which forced me to evaluate my academic, professional and personal experiences. I had to draw upon these to outline my professional beliefs succinctly. Here's what I wrote:

I believe that educational leadership is a vehicle for addressing some of the inequalities of our society, both at a micro level within the school community and at a macro level within the wider community. Harris (2008) argues that school leaders have a 'moral imperative' to address the widening gap between the poorest and most affluent students, although it is my view that school leadership goes beyond this. Schools should not simply serve as a sorting system for the economic purposes of a nation; rather, schools are charged with contributing to the development of future citizens of a democratic society. Dempster (2009) contends that learning is 'the means through which individuals can change their lives'. The concept of learning being a powerful tool in transforming lives underpins my professional beliefs about education. It is my belief that schools should:

- *improve the outcomes of students academically, personally and socially, adding value to the lives of young people*
- *value and recognise individuals within the school community, providing the necessary support and challenge to develop all stakeholders*
- *be centres of learning for all stakeholders and exercise a positive influence in and on the wider community.*

These beliefs were shaped by my own experiences. My education afforded me with both the qualifications and qualities I needed to build a life that made a positive contribution to society. I was given opportunities to make progress as a professional, realising and developing my potential capacity for leadership. My career as a teacher continues to provide me with opportunities for personal and academic growth, while potentially serving as a role model within the wider community.

I wish I could have articulated this as clearly when I first started teaching but, with hindsight, I recognise how my thinking was forged by the experiences I had had inside and outside of the classroom up until this point. I knew I wanted to help young people; that was the *what*. I knew I needed to be a great teacher and leader; that was the *how*. But if you had asked me *why* in 2006, I would have struggled to explain myself.

Back in 2006, I was a cover supervisor in a challenging school in South London. I had just graduated from university, and this was my first proper job. It was supposed to be just a stopgap until I could secure a job working in the media. My role entailed providing cover for classes where teachers were absent. And there was a lot of teacher absence. My line manager was a lovely Irish woman named Miriam Whittington; a kind and gentle soul who worked in the admin team, managing cover across the school. She would often have an apologetic look on her face each morning as she explained my cover for the day.

She knew behaviour was poor and absence was high, which meant the job was tough. The school was struggling to retain teachers, let alone cover staff, so I think she was conflicted giving me classes she knew would be challenging – but she had no option. She gave me a Year 10 science cover. Year 10 displayed notoriously bad behaviour, but were also, on paper, a bright cohort. I waited in the classroom for the end of break. I remember feeling a mix of excitement and raw terror at the prospect of being responsible for the class, but I soon learned that I thrived on the pressure.

I stood by the door and greeted students cheerfully as they entered the room. I asked them to take off their bags and to take their seats. Two particularly boisterous lads came to the door, and my spidey-sense tingled. I felt like these boys were influential, strolling in later than everyone else; louder than everyone else; a little more confident than everyone else. I asked them their names and directed them to sit at the front. Immediately they questioned why. I made some corny joke and they complied. I took the register and explained I had few rules: I will treat you with courtesy and respect and I expect the same. I explained the cover task, but I could tell from the questions I initially received that the students did not recognise the topic: they had never been taught it.

Internally, I wanted to scream. I felt like I had been set up to fail. How was I going to cover a class that didn't know what they were being asked to do? Surely, that would be a recipe for disaster. The kids would kick off. I would not be able to control their behaviour. I would get the sack. But there was another nagging feeling: frustration that these students were being set up to fail too. I got the attention of the class, who had started to become restless, and I announced that we would learn it together.

'I am not an expert, but we will go through it together. We will learn this together as a class.'

And we did. We muddled through the material. I can't remember the content of the lesson, but I remember using analogies to explain something in the textbook and the class erupting with laughter. I used an example familiar to the students to explain a scientific concept described in the curriculum. The students completed their tasks. The behaviour was not terrible. At the end of the lesson, I dismissed the class and some thanked me. It left me with this combination of feelings: a sense of accomplishment, a feeling of pride and a growing sense of indignation. I wanted to make sure that I could teach the content clearly and be confident that what I was teaching was accurate. I felt a little bit angry that the young people were being given such a raw deal. I wanted to help these young people. Without realising it, I had stumbled on my *why*; albeit a fuzzy, abstract version of it.

In his book *Start With Why*, Simon Sinek (2009) argues that, when an individual or organisation can effectively articulate their purpose and the reason they exist and behave as they do, it inspires action. It took me several years to be able to express succinctly the reason why I am a teacher, but I think I would have benefited greatly if I was taken through this process at the outset of my career. It would have served as both a mission statement to aspire to and an encouragement during challenging periods in my career.

What is your origin story?

So what is your origin story? Why are you a teacher? This is an important question for you to consider. The answer is at the core of who you show up as in the classroom and beyond. It's the engine that drives you, and understanding this will unlock the key to maintaining motivation in one of the most rewarding and taxing professions.

Spark something

Start with why

The origin story is cherished in popular culture. It allows us to get beneath the surface of what motivates and drives our favourite heroes and villains. For example, *Breaking Bad*'s prequel *Better Call Saul* and Disney's *Mufasa* offer insights into how the protagonist was shaped and moulded into their character. Understanding their formative experiences provides a framework for understanding why they see the world in the way that they do, especially in moments of difficulty. Reconnecting to why you started and / or the factors that influenced you to start is a powerful catalyst to provide clarity and focus.

Writing a pen portrait can be challenging because it requires you to try to be objective in evaluating your experiences, beliefs and values. Just as an artist might begin a self-portrait by beginning with sketching a circle to help accurately establish the facial proportions, there are some questions that can help you to begin sketching the contours of your identity, before adding more layers of detail.

To begin, you will need to start with your professional CV. How you complete this is up to you: you might want to work through each question and write a summary paragraph, or you may prefer to grab a big sheet of paper and create a mind map. Answer the following questions (Campbell et al., 2003) to help develop the initial picture of who you are as a professional:

- Where and when were you educated as a teacher? (Give the dates and location.)
- What qualifications do you have? (State the awards and dates.)
- What teaching experience do you have?
- What areas of the curriculum have you taught? (List the subject areas you have taught, along with details of age groups.)
- What posts of responsibility have you held? (List posts you have been promoted to, and their responsibilities.)
- What external responsibilities have you had?
- What professional-development activities and processes have you been involved in? (List and provide dates and durations of activities. Give details of whether you contributed to or led any of these.)
- What interests in education do you have? (List your current and past interests, and any non-teaching activities or part-time teaching in other contexts that could support your development.)
- Are there any other related interests or experiences that enhance your profile?
- List any external roles that you have undertaken, such as examiner or moderator.

Once you have completed your CV, you might already start seeing some patterns or trends emerge. Perhaps you have enjoyed working in environments that put you under pressure, or maybe you have flourished working with a coach or mentor. It can be really rewarding to revisit moments in your origin story that reveal strengths and weaknesses, and aptitudes and talents you did not know you possessed. Whatever this exercise has helped you capture, it will now form the basis of the next part: the portrait. Use the following questions to help you craft your pen portrait:

- What kind of teacher are you?
- What are your core beliefs about teaching and learning?
- How would you describe your teaching style?
- What makes you tick as a teacher? What motivates you to develop your teaching?

- What ideas do you have about the nature of teaching? What do these ideas add to knowledge about teaching?
- Where do your ideas and beliefs about teaching and learning historically come from?
- How did you come to these ideas?
- What helped you formulate your ideas and thinking about teaching?
- Do your practices accord with current views of teaching? If not, how are they different?
- Do you address inequalities and discrimination in education?
- What do you feel strongly about in education?

Now you have outlined your professional and personal journey, you should be better able to articulate not only your origin story, but why you are a teacher.

CHAPTER 2
PICK 'N' MIX

Great teachers are a unique blend

Nostalgia from the 90s

Before its demise in 2009, Woolworths was a popular store on British High Streets. Affectionately nicknamed Woolies, it was well known for selling pick 'n' mix sweets. Black jacks, rhubarb and custard, strawberry pencils, fruit salads, cola bottles – the choice of confectionery was vast and wide-ranging. It meant that every customer would approach the counter with a unique blend of sweets, sporting different flavours, colours and shapes in their paper bags. No sweet bag was the same because it was determined by the individual's selection.

Memories of visits to the pick 'n' mix section in Woolies fill my mind with a sense of nostalgia; that, and the TV shows I watched as a child. I didn't realise it then, but they were shaping my beliefs about who and what teachers should be. Perhaps you grew up on more recent representations of school life, such as *Waterloo Road*, *High School Musical* and *The Inbetweeners*. I grew up watching *Grange Hill*, *The Fresh Prince of Bel-Air* and *Saved by the Bell*.

Teaching on the silver screen

I always find depictions of teachers in the media intriguing, but the most impactful iterations were those found in *To Sir, with love*, *Dead Poets Society*, *Sister Act 2* and *Freedom Writers*. These are a few of my favourite films that have graced the silver screen with narratives centred around what happens in the classroom. Some are based in affluent private schools; others in underfunded state schools. In some, the teacher is cool and able to relate to their students with ease. In most, the teacher struggles initially to connect with their classes. In each, the narrative arc builds momentum to a peak where the conflict is resolved by the students excelling; becoming better versions of themselves.

In *To Sir, wth Love*, Denham would never otherwise have considered himself becoming a boxing instructor. Todd would never have found the courage to stand for what was right in *Dead Poets Society*. The children of St Francis Academy would never have won the choir competition and kept their school open in *Sister Act 2*, and the real events depicted in *Freedom Writers* show that the students of Woodrow Wilson High School would never have understood the Holocaust and the implications of prejudice. Each protagonist of these films competes with forces known and unknown, visible and invisible, that seek to push and / or pull their students in a particular direction.

Breaking the stereotype

Despite the stereotypes we often observe in the media, in reality there is no distinct mould that all teachers are formed from. Hargreaves (1992) argues that:

> Teachers teach in the way they do not just because of the skills they have or have not learned. The ways they teach are also grounded in their backgrounds, their biographies, in the kinds of teachers they have become. Their careers – their hopes and dreams, their opportunities and aspirations, or the frustration of these things – are also important for teachers' commitment, enthusiasm and morale.

Every teacher is a combination, a compound, a composite of varying factors – like a bag of pick 'n' mix. There is no identikit for teachers; an assembly line producing people lacking variety or individuality. You might be able to mass-produce cola bottles that look and taste exactly the same, but it doesn't work like that for humans. The human element is what makes education the wonderful, unpredictable, messy, fulfilling process it is. The adult human you place in a classroom to teach younger humans is a large determinant for the outcomes the school produces.

So, if teachers are not mass produced, what is the key ingredient that all teachers share?

Well, it's not just business; it's personal. There is a really personal element to those who pursue teaching as a vocation. Like seriously, who would be a teacher? If you were to write a job description for the average classroom teacher, it might read like this:

Overview:

Are you a results-driven professional seeking an exhilarating role that demands multitasking, adaptability and boundless creativity? Join our dynamic educational team as a classroom teacher, where you will face challenges to rival any high-stakes business environment.

Responsibilities:

1. *Educational Strategist: Develop and implement lesson plans that align with academic standards, while fostering critical-thinking and problem-solving skills.*
2. *Performance Analyst: Assess and track student progress using data-driven methods to optimise learning outcomes.*
3. *Classroom Operations Manager: Oversee day-to-day classroom operations, resources and technology, ensuring a smooth and efficient learning environment.*
4. *Stakeholder Liaison: Foster strong relationships with students, parents / carers and colleagues through effective communication and collaboration.*
5. *Crisis Management Consultant: Navigate diverse challenges, from academic struggles to behavioural issues, with proactive and innovative solutions, maintaining composure in high-pressure situations.*

Requirements:

- *A Bachelor's degree in Education or a related field, with a track record of academic achievement*
- *Exceptional organisational skills akin to managing a high-profile project*
- *Strong analytical capabilities to interpret data and tailor teaching strategies to individual student needs*
- *Outstanding interpersonal skills for seamless stakeholder engagement and conflict resolution*
- *The ability to thrive in a fast-paced, ever-evolving environment while maintaining a high level of professionalism.*

This role offers the thrill of high-stakes challenges and the opportunity to make a lasting impact on the future generation's success. If you're ready to tackle these challenges head-on and enhance our team, apply now and join our mission.

When you reflect on the reality of being a teacher, it seems like an improbable assignment. Therefore, those who embark on employment as an educator must have some personal vested interest. Day (2012) argues that there is 'an unavoidable interrelationship between the personal and the professional … teaching demands significant personal investment'. Even if you have wanted to be a teacher ever since you read about Miss Honey in Roald Dahl's *Matilda* (1988), your professional ambitions are not easily detached from your personal motivations.

Personally, I suspect this is one reason the profession is sometimes taken for granted; many who enter teaching do so because of their strong sense of vocation. This commitment endures even though the wider conditions surrounding the profession have not always made teaching an easy choice.

The fact is that 'significant personal investment is the bedrock on which effective teachers are developed'. It is on this foundation that a 'dedicated, highly competent teaching force ... working together for the continuous betterment of schools' can be built (Fullan, 2003a). In one way, your specific background is somewhat irrelevant to whether you can become an effective teacher. Every teacher is a unique blend of both 'selfish and unselfish motives' (Fullan, 2003b).

You see, it's not all altruistic.

When I joined my first school, I wanted to help equip young people from my local area with skills to help them forge a future (unselfish) so I could take personal satisfaction in being part of their journey (selfish). I wanted to be 'the boy done good' from my estate (selfish) to be a beacon for others trying to escape poverty (unselfish). When I returned as a teacher to my childhood secondary school, I wanted to become a legend like the teachers who taught me (selfish) to create positive outcomes, experiences and core memories for young people who were like me (unselfish).

Teachers are a funny breed. They are rare, unique and valuable. This is the reason why not everybody can or should be a teacher. In my experience, amazing, effective teachers come in all colours, shapes and sizes; different temperaments and personalities, political persuasions and beliefs. But the very best teachers I have encountered, both personally and professionally, share 'a professional commitment to improving the lives of people through education' (Dempster, 2009a). If you share this commitment, regardless of your unique blend, you have the essential ingredient necessary to make a difference in the lives of young people.

Spark something

Pick 'n' mix

The analogy of pick 'n' mix should hopefully convey the sense that all teachers are an assortment of beliefs, experiences and many other factors that shape our personalities. The famous teachers of film and screen approached their work in different ways, but always with the same objective.

To be a teacher is to recognise the professional commitment to improve lives through education, but that will look different in every person. Understanding how and why you show up the way you do is not only helpful, but can provide you with valuable insights into how to channel your unique dispositions into a force that impacts others.

A tool that was helpful for me to understand how my personality interacts with my work is the Insights Discovery® colours tool. You answer a series of questions and it produces a psychometric profile that offers insights into personal style; key strengths and weaknesses; the value you bring to a team; possible blind spots; and areas for development.

You are assigned a colour profile that matches your responses:

- **Fiery Red:** action-oriented, determined and focused
- **Sunshine Yellow:** sociable, enthusiastic and persuasive
- **Earth Green:** caring, patient and supportive
- **Cool Blue:** analytical, precise and critical-thinking.

It made me realise that, while we are all unique as individuals, there are distinct patterns that emerge among people who share similar profiles. I have worked with colleagues who fit every one of those different colour profiles. Developing greater self-awareness about my strengths and weaknesses helped me to be a better teacher. It also helped me have a greater sense of how to work with others, given their particular dispositions. It allowed me to develop an awareness of blind spots that naturally emerge as a result of my particular profile. What was particularly useful was exploring the contrast between how one shows up on a 'good day' versus on a 'bad day'.

From my experience, the Insights Discovery colours tool does come with a cost. It's usually delivered across an organisation by a team, although there are opportunities for private individuals to complete the profile. There are free versions online, which are not as robust but provide a basic colour profile. There is also a great book, *Surrounded by Idiots: The Four Types of Human Behaviour and How to Effectively Communicate with Each in Business (and in Life)* by Thomas Erikson (2025). In his book, he unpacks some of the ideas linked to the colour profiles in a witty and practical way.

I personally prefer Insights Discovery as a tool because I like the way the profile is set out, but there are many other well-regarded tools available that offer similar insights, including:

Myers-Briggs Type Indicator® (MBTI®): a questionnaire that assesses a person's personality type, preferences and strengths; the MBTI assigns a four-letter result, which corresponds to four categories:

- Introversion (I) or Extraversion (E)
- Sensing (S) or iNtuition (N)
- Thinking (T) or Feeling (F)
- Judging (J) or Perceiving (P).

DiSC® assessment: a personality assessment that categorises a person's behaviours and personality styles into four distinct types:

- Dominance
- Influence
- Steadiness
- Compliance / Conscientiousness.

I have personally used all three tools, although I did not come across these tools until I became a middle leader. I think that having such insights would have helped me develop as a teacher and leader. At the core of any of these tools is the goal of gaining a greater sense of self-awareness that, in turn, supports our work in the classroom and beyond.

CHAPTER 3
MINDSET MATTERS

Great teachers believe in potential

Blind to potential

Now most head teachers are chosen because they possess a number of fine qualities. They understand children and they have the children's best interests at heart. They are sympathetic. They are fair and they are deeply interested in education. Miss Trunchbull possessed none of these qualities and how she got her present job was a mystery.

Dahl (1988)

Roald Dahl's fictional Agatha Trunchbull in *Matilda* stands out in children's literature for her total ineptitude in realising the potential of the students of Crunchem Hall Primary School. Aside from her unsafe and unsavoury practices of tossing children by their pigtails, locking kids in the chokey and forcing students to gorge themselves on sickly chocolate cake, she lacks the vision to imagine a different, improved reality for the children in her charge. It is far easier to crunch 'em, to crush and subjugate the children, that they might accept their lot in life and assume their stations without resistance. She fails to recognise the potential of the children in front of her, even when confronted with a most exceptional child: Matilda.

Surely such people exist only in fiction, right?

You would be surprised. Here are excerpts from school reports of some well-known figures:

He must devote less of his time to sport if he wants to be a success ... You can't make a living out of football.

Gary Lineker's school report, City of Leicester Boys' School

That is from the school report of Gary Lineker, the 1986 and 1992 English Footballer of the Year, 1986 FIFA World Cup Golden Boot Winner, 1987–88 Spanish Cup

Winner, 1991 FA Cup Winner and host of the BBC football programme *Match of the Day* for more than two decades.

Judi would be a very good pupil if she lived in this world.

Hurley (2002)

According to her teacher, Judi's extensive imagination caused her to fall short of being a very good pupil. However, it was possibly a key factor in establishing Dame Judith Dench as one of Britain's greatest actresses, with a career spanning over six decades on stage, television and film, and an Academy Award, a Tony Award, two Golden Globe Awards, four British Academy Television Awards, six British Academy Film Awards and seven Olivier Awards.

Hopeless. Rather a clown in class. He is just wasting other pupils' time. Certainly on the road to failure.

John Lennon's school report from Quarry Bank School, Liverpool

This was the school report of English singer, songwriter and musician John Lennon, who gained worldwide fame as the founder, co-songwriter, co-lead vocalist and rhythm guitarist of the Beatles.

He will never amount to anything.

Albert Einstein's school report from Luitpold Gymnasium, Munich

Written by his Munich schoolmaster in 1895, Albert Einstein's teacher could not envisage Einstein amounting to *anything*, let alone becoming some kind of Einstein. He probably could not imagine a day when his student's name would become synonymous with genius.

My point is not to vilify the teachers of these famous alumni, or even to hold up their achievements as the standard of success. Rather, my goal is to draw attention to the factors that may have unwittingly shaped these teachers' responses towards their students; to consider how their mindsets influenced how they performed their professional responsibilities.

Mindset matters.

Growth vs fixed mindset

Mindset is an invisible force that drives a number of our responses. Professor Carol Dweck of Stanford University is known for her work on mindset and motivation (Dweck, 2012). At this point, you have probably heard about the importance of having a *growth mindset* rather than a *fixed mindset*; the latter often used in a pejorative manner when describing a person. However, the theory is less about labelling or categorising people and more about exploring our relationship with intelligence and how this influences our motivation.

In essence, Dweck's research found that those employing a growth mindset believe that:

- intelligence, personality and abilities are open to development
- effort makes the difference
- failure is an opportunity to learn
- their focus should be on improving,

whereas those employing a fixed mindset believe that:

- intelligence, personality and abilities are fixed
- the more effort you have to put in, the less your ability
- failure is catastrophic
- their focus should be on proving.

Why does this matter for teachers? Dweck found that 'teachers with the fixed mindset created an atmosphere of judging. These teachers looked at students' beginning performance and decided who was smart and who was dumb. Then they gave up on the "dumb" ones' (Dweck, 2012). How many schoolchildren have had this as their experience of the education system in the most formative years of their lives?

I have a bitter memory from the second year of my A-levels. We were having some sort of 'preparation for university' session. It was a short while before it was my turn to have my one-to-one tutorial with my form tutor. I cannot remember a lot of what we discussed. We talked about my most recent test results and teacher report. I remember his exasperation and frustration with me, and I recall him saying 'Christian, with grades like these, no university will want you'. His words stung. No, they pierced me. I may have even recoiled at hearing them. Those were his parting words before he moved on to his next student.

He had stated the brutal facts. I do not deny that: I was not fulfilling my potential. However, in his delivery of what I can only imagine he saw as 'tough love', he offered no hope, no counsel, no compassion, no empathy, no unwavering faith that things could and would be better. I returned to my seat and wondered why I had even bothered to make the 90-minute journey to school. He had confirmed what I was struggling not to believe: that I was a failure and there was no remedy.

As an adult, school leader and parent, I look back at that experience with incredulity, but I understand how mindset may have been at play in that circumstance. In contrast to fixed-mindset teachers, Dweck found that teachers with a growth mindset 'created an atmosphere of trust, not judgment. These teachers believed in the growth of the intellect and talent, and they were fascinated with the process of learning both for themselves and their students' (Dweck, 2012).

I wonder how my form tutor's conversation with me all those years ago might have gone had he employed a growth mindset: 'Christian, at present, with grades like these, no university will want you. You are not fulfilling your potential yet. Let's discuss some strategies to help you demonstrate your true ability.' Implicit in this imagined conversation is a belief in the potential to develop, to grow, to learn, to excel. It doesn't ignore the reality, but it is imbued with a hopefulness that things can be better. In his book *Good to Great: Why Some Companies Make the Leap... and Others Don't*, Jim Collins describes how great organisations 'confront the brutal facts without losing unwavering faith'.

This has to be what schools do. I believe this can happen only if the teachers in the classrooms employ mindsets that have faith in the possibilities of potential. It doesn't matter how inspirational, charismatic, efficient or effective a headteacher is if her staff body employs a mindset that writes some children off. Harris (2008) argues that 'the influence of heads ... on pupils' academic learning will almost always be mediated through adults'. Mindset matters.

Much has been said about mindset in recent years; as often happens in education, a new concept grows in popularity and fads emerge. Dweck has since written about the issues with developing a false growth mindset and other misconceptions. Nonetheless, in my view, the core tenet of being a teacher necessitates a mindset that sees intelligence as something that can be developed. We have high expectations only of those we have high hopes for.

In one of my favourite films, *The Pursuit of Happyness*, there is a scene that illustrates the importance of mindset. The protagonist, Chris Gardner, is playing a casual game of basketball with his son after school. His son expresses his desire to 'go pro' as he shoots the ball. In the film, Gardner immediately responds by explaining to his son why it is highly unlikely he will become a professional athlete. He cites his own mediocrity at sport as a reason why his son should give up on pursuing a sporting career. Disheartened, his son ceases to play and begins to pack away.

Reflecting on his words, their impact and the mindset it belies, Gardner exhorts his son, saying:

Hey. Don't ever let somebody tell you you can't do something, not even me. Alright? You got a dream, you gotta protect it. People can't do something themselves, they want to tell you you can't do it. If you want something, go get it. Period.

The type of teachers we need to populate classrooms are fundamentally people who echo this sentiment; those who extol effort and see failure as an opportunity to learn; those who believe in the power of potential. In the movie, Gardner appears to recognise the incongruity in declaring his son's potential as limited and fixed, at the same time as seeking to develop his own. It is my view that it is harder to see the potential in others if one has not yet realised the potential in oneself.

Spark something

Mindset matters

When I first came across Dweck's research, it resonated with me. She articulated something about how our beliefs shape our behaviour. I have worked with colleagues in the past who have spoken about children in ways that suggested those children would be consigned to failure. Rather than serving as a change agent in the classroom, these colleagues actually helped accelerate the self-fulfilling prophecies some of their students carried. Their beliefs about the young people shaped their expectations and, in turn, their expectations to a large extent shaped the performance of the young people.

At the heart of Dweck's work on mindset is an exploration of beliefs about **ability**, **effort** and **change**. In my view, these aspects are active ingredients in learning, and our beliefs about them shape the way we engage with others; namely, young people.

Let's take the example of a class of children: they arrive at your class with prior attainment indicating different levels of ability. While their prior attainment provides some initial data on their aptitude at a specified point in time, it cannot comprehensively or exhaustively tell you everything there is to know about their **ability**. Their potential is unknowable. Your job is, through the vehicle of teaching and learning, to help them make progress from their starting point to a desired outcome. You seek to bring about **change**. A great deal of your ability to bring about change depends on a multiplier that makes their potential unknowable: **effort**. The combined efforts of both student and teacher can have unexpected, wonderful outcomes.

It's what makes results days such a joy as a professional; seeing young people reap the rewards of their labour, experiencing a better, alternate future than their prior attainment might have predicted. A teacher seeking to develop a growth mindset within their students places greater emphasis on effort, recognising that ability is open to development. I think it is important for teachers to have real-life effort narratives to help shape high expectations. These could be narratives that illustrate how the efforts of a young person under your tutelage achieved great outcomes. More powerful still is a personal story of your own effort narrative, where your effort made the difference. By providing students with a real-life example from your own life and / or another young person who sat where they sit, you offer them a vision of where they could be if they adopt a mindset geared towards growth.

Here are some questions to help you develop your own effort narrative:

1. **Set the scene: the struggle**
    - What is a learning activity you found difficult at first?
    - How did you feel about it before you started?
    - What made this activity particularly challenging for you?

2. **The mindset shift: employing effort**
    - What did you do when you realised the activity was difficult?
    - Did you ever consider giving up? What stopped you?
    - What were the strategies or habits that helped you persevere, or who were the people who helped you persevere?

3. **The outcome: reflecting on the result**
    - What were the outcomes as a result of your effort?
    - Reflecting back, what did you learn about yourself?
    - How did your effort change the way you saw yourself?

4. **The message: mindset matters**
    - What does this narrative show about the importance of effort?
    - How might this narrative encourage a student who is struggling?
    - What would you go back and say to your younger self at the start of this experience?

PART 2
CAPACITY

PART 2

CHAPTER 4
LEARN YOUR CRAFT

Great teachers earn their stripes

Quelling quiet quitting

In August 2018, Nigerian singer Burna Boy released his song 'Ye', and in doing so captured the zeitgeist of a generation. He sings about how he cannot come and kill himself for work. This describes a general contemporary attitude towards work. For many in Gen Z, unlike the Boomers, Gen Xers and Millennials before them, work is not something they should kill themselves for. Following the Covid-19 pandemic and the move towards working from home, quiet quitting has become the order of the day. And I am not advocating an unhealthy relationship with work, especially in teaching. It is a profession that can be all-consuming: a teacher's job is never complete.

I know the experience of making a to-do list and still having tasks incomplete. I know the experience of arriving at work early with the best of intentions and having my plans derailed by the unexpected events of the day. While many teachers share this experience, I do not think that heavy workloads are unique to the profession. However, the specific nuances of a teacher's workload are vastly different from the challenges of somebody working in retail or construction or any other industry. There is much still to be done in education to ameliorate some of the practices that often make teaching unattractive, undesirable and untenable as a career path for graduates. I will say more on this later in the book.

No pain, no gain

My point is that teaching isn't just a job that one can do haphazardly. Given that we have established the necessary moral imperative that one should possess to be an effective educator, a great teacher has to be prepared to do the work, to put in the hard graft, to earn their stripes. In my opinion, it is not a career path that one can quietly quit. There is too much at stake. Children and young people should not be failed in securing a meaningful education because of apathy on their teacher's part. There will be occasions, seasons, periods that are challenging, difficult and exhausting. November is always going to be one of the toughest months to teach through: it is the nature of the beast.

But the beast can be slain. Or at least tamed. The problem is that, increasingly, too few people persevere to discover this. I am not having a go at people who leave the profession. The levels of teacher attrition are a macro issue that can only be addressed at scale by constructive government policies and strategic leadership across the sector. I am speaking more about the expectation that teaching would be, and perhaps should be, easy. Research suggests that, during periods of economic instability and uncertainty, more people join the profession, seeing it as a safe bet. Yes, teaching does provide a level of job security, opportunities for career progression and the reward of shaping young lives. And oh, the holidays, the holidays!

It should also come with a warning label: teaching is not for the faint of heart. Along with some of those selfish motivations we've talked about, there must also be a winning mentality to be the best. There should be a thirst to develop and grow and thrive personally and professionally; otherwise, what credibility do you have to stand in front of impressionable young people and attempt to get them to do the same? Teachers must be life-long learners, if that is what they seek to produce in their classrooms.

Rotter (1966) argues that an individual's motivation goes beyond their experiences or environment. He designates individuals as having either an external or internal locus of control, which reflects whether the subject believes reward follows from 'his own behaviour or attributes versus the degree to which he feels the reward is controlled by forces outside of himself' (Rotter, 1966). Part of learning the craft of teaching is recognising one's own agency to effect change.

This is not to ignore the impact working conditions can have. In the USA, Czubaj (1996) found that, when working conditions of teachers remained conducive to the interactive dynamics of motivation, highly motivated teachers taught students to become highly motivated themselves. Teachers modelled and transferred their mode of motivation to their students so that teachers with extrinsic modes of motivation passed on a 'form of motivation burdened with stress, anxiety and low self-esteem' (Czubaj, 1996). Stress, anxiety and low self-esteem are not good cheerleaders. They do not generate the type of drive, thirst for knowledge or curiosity found in lifelong learners. Such learners learn because they want to learn; not just because of the outcome or external reward.

Don't misunderstand me: student outcomes change lives. SATs matter. GCSEs matter. A-levels matter. Whether you agree with it or not, this is the education system we have in the UK, and these are the parameters schools work within. We need teachers who understand that the true reward of learning is the learning itself – and the person you become as you are imbued with a greater depth of knowledge, skills and understanding. They serve as tried and tested veterans who have themselves been subjected to the messy, frustrating, rewarding process of learning, and continue to do so as they learn their craft.

For instance, Rose and Medway (1981) found that teachers with an internal locus of control tended to have classes of higher achieving students than teachers with an external locus of control. Results showed that teachers with an internal locus of control 'seemed to encourage internally controlled expectancies on the part of the students' (Rose and Medway, 1981). Rose and Medway emphasise that students' locus of control is generally a good predictor of achievement. It would appear that, in a transactional teaching relationship, teachers potentially transmit their particular locus of control to students.

'Come back tomorrow'

In the 1984 film *Karate Kid*, teenager Daniel LaRusso desires to learn karate in order to defend himself from bullies. He asks the eccentric handyman from his apartment building, Mr Miyagi, to teach him karate. Mr Miyagi agrees and sets Daniel a number of menial chores to complete: washing and waxing cars, sanding the floor, painting the fence, painting the house. After a number of days, working tirelessly without seeing how his efforts remotely connect to his desire to learn karate, Daniel is ready to pack it all in and confronts Mr Miyagi. In one of the best-known sequences, Mr Miyagi demonstrates that Daniel's repetition of the chores helps him develop the muscle memory required for defensive blocks. Having proven to Daniel how the seeming drudgery of his chores are actually causing Daniel to learn the craft, Mr Miyagi tells him, 'Come back tomorrow.'

Before this scene, Daniel would have concluded 'I can't come and kill myself' working like an enslaved person, when what he really wanted was to learn karate. Unbeknown to him, he *was* learning; it was just hard and frustrating and slow. He needed to be resilient, determined and 'come back tomorrow'. If he quit, he would lose out on learning karate. If he decided to quiet-quit, he would waste his energy, time and opportunity. He needed to commit to the process of learning. He had to earn his stripes. He had to go through the grind. There were no shortcuts to his sense of self-efficacy.

It's the same with teaching.

Your credibility to lead learning is that you yourself continue to be a learner. The data on teacher attrition is stark, particularly for new teachers. The figures show that in 2024, 42,200 teachers left state-funded teaching for reasons other than retirement. Around one in 10 early-career teachers quit after their first few years at the chalkface. It saddens me, because the teaching profession is haemorrhaging talent and has done for several years now. While it is my view that the responsibility for this lies with policymakers, I feel as a profession we must help to manage the expectations of those joining the teaching workforce. Teaching is the most rewarding profession there is; there are few others that have such an impact on the flourishing of humanity. Nevertheless, teachers must earn their stripes.

Spark something

Learn your craft

Learning any craft can be painful because it sucks to suck. Nobody enjoys being bad at something, yet it is a necessary part of becoming good. Many who train to teach expecting quickly to be effective practitioners in the classroom often end up disappointed and disillusioned. The process of growing in competence is often long and arduous, especially when constant, repeated failure (or the sense of it) batters your self-image. Nothing can make you feel inadequate like an unruly class or a group of children who still do not understand concepts you have taught, bringing the best of your A-game.

In management literature, the four stages of competence are well known:

Stage 1: Unconscious incompetence	We don't know or understand what it takes to be a great teacher. We possibly know from experience what receiving great teaching feels like, but doing it is another matter.
Stage 2: Conscious incompetence	Even though we do not have all the skills under our belt, we are aware of our areas of development and how they will support our growth as professionals.
Stage 3: Conscious competence	We know how to employ a particular skill or aspect of pedagogy, but we have to be deliberate and intentional in doing it. The skill isn't yet second nature, and if we stop we revert back to sucking at said activity.
Stage 4: Unconscious competence	We now just do the thing automatically. We don't even think about it. It 'just comes naturally'. Not only do we no longer suck, but we make the skill look easy – like we've always had the ability.

I think a lot of early-career teachers eject during stages 2 and 3. *The job feels all-consuming. The kids don't listen. It's just too hard.* If that sounds familiar and you feel like giving up, similar to the Karate Kid, allow me to be your Mr Miyagi for a moment: film yourself. I know this is common practice for many trainee teachers, but I believe it is a helpful practice for all teachers at whatever career stage.

Think about one aspect of your pedagogy you want to develop and record yourself. Once you have a short segment of your teaching captured on film, analyse it like an athlete would a match replay. It is surprising how powerful reviewing footage can be. It forces you to make judgements and conclusions based on evidence. Invite trusted colleagues to review the material with you. Elite athletes pore over footage of past performances to glean key insights and enhance future performance. In a similar way, identifying and observing strengths and areas for development supercharges our ability to improve and develop as practitioners.

The biggest hurdle with learning any craft is that it involves a tolerance for failure, which we are generally not great with. In his book *Black Box Thinking*, Matthew Syed (2016) argues that a method for achieving high performance involves embracing failure as a learning tool. Just as the black boxes in aircrafts record flight data, allowing for analysis of mistakes and failures to improve aviation safety, so too does a 'Black Box' mindset recognise that failure is an opportunity for growth and development. In short, a big part of learning any craft involves the ability to tolerate 'sucking' temporarily as you develop competence.

CHAPTER 5
GETTING THINGS DONE

Great teachers make things happen

Game changers

On 18 December 2022, one of the most epic games of football took place as Argentina and France took to the pitch in the World Cup final. There were many twists and turns throughout the match as both teams fought for supremacy. Both teams consisted of top-class players in their own right, but there were two players in particular that gripped the attention of the world: Argentina's Lionel Messi and France's Kylian Mbappe.

In that match, Messi scored twice; Mbappe, three times. There seemed to be a private battle between the former teammates; the outgoing king versus the newly crowned prince. Mbappe sought a second World Cup trophy for France, while Messi sought his elusive first. Each served as talisman for their footballing nation. Fans from both countries could be confident that while their star player was on the pitch, success was attainable. Mbappe brought his team back from the brink, scoring two goals in quick succession. In the end, the outgoing Argentine king was able to better the French prince.

There is something about having someone in your midst who demonstrates high levels of competence and skill. If that player is on your team, it breeds confidence. If they are on the opposing team, it creates fear. For great athletes, their confidence emanates from a secure sense of their capabilities. They have a sense of their own agency: they can make things happen. It is essential that teachers also have a sense of their own agency, as leaders of learning.

Hargreaves (2009) rightly argues that teachers are the 'ultimate arbiters of change ... the classroom door is the gateway to implementation or the drawbridge that holds it at bay'. When a teacher closes their classroom door to teach the young people in their charge, it is a little like when a football manager sends his players onto the pitch. It's down to the players. The manager can make structural changes, provide insights and feedback at key points, as well as cheer, cajole and scold from the sidelines, but the success of the team largely depends on the performance of the players. Likewise, a headteacher depends on the efficacy of the teachers.

Building agency

But how do teachers develop agency? Priestley (2015) outlines the following three aspects:

> First, agency is rooted in past experience; and individuals with a wide repertoire of experience may achieve agency more readily than those without. Secondly, agency is always oriented to the future through the setting of goals and the ability to envisage future possibilities; in this case, people who are able to imagine multiple trajectories are likely to achieve agency more readily than those who are limited in their aspirations. Third, agency is always acted on in the present, shaped by both what is actually possible given existing resources and constraints and judgements about what is possible.

It is no surprise to me that Messi and Mbappe stood out that night in December. As a child, Messi played football in the streets of Rosario, Argentina's third-largest city. Similarly, Mbappe started to develop his trade in the streets of deprived Parisian suburb Bondy. These humble beginnings undoubtedly provided them with a repertoire of past experiences they were able to draw on and bring to bear in Qatar. Having previously won footballing awards at the highest levels, they could both envisage a future in which their home nation secured football's most coveted prize. This sense of agency shaped what they did in the present.

It follows that teachers also require a wide range of experiences to develop a sense of agency. While I recognise the necessity to retain and nurture the teachers we have currently in the profession and those joining, I fear that, for new teachers, there is a danger of being mollycoddled; providing too narrow an experience of teaching that contrasts starkly with the realities. From my own personal experience, I remember being allocated a challenging group of disillusioned, disaffected and academically weak Year 10 students. It was a really tough gig. I struggled with managing their behaviour and, at the time, would have much rather been given an 'easier' set of children to teach.

Leading from the front

But it wasn't the class. It was me.

I had a class of academically able Year 8 students and I struggled to manage their behaviour too. The two groups misbehaved for different reasons and in different ways. I was on 'swampy ground' and would have much preferred to be on 'firm ground'. Garratt (2005) suggests that 'it is the area of swampy ground that offers the greatest opportunities and challenges'. I longed for the firm ground of polite, well-behaved, academically engaged students – every teacher's dream. But I quickly learned that it is rare for students to arrive at the classroom in this form; rather, such classes are crafted and cultivated by the teacher.

I learned the hard way that teachers are leaders. They really are. It isn't something quaint to say to colleagues without a formal teaching and learning role or responsibility. Teachers must envisage the future possibility of the young people in their charge succeeding, which, in turn, guides their actions in the present. It is what Schön (1995) describes as reflection-in-action, perpetually reflecting on our practice and making the necessary adjustments in the moment.

There were so many options I had available to me that I had not exercised. I spoke to the students, collectively and individually, reiterating my expectations. I contacted their homes to elicit parental support. I amended seating plans, moving key students closer to me. I spoke to other colleagues about specific students and identified the most effective pedagogy. I provided greater scaffolding to support less able students and provided more challenge to more able students. I observed specific students in other classes and settings. I made rewarding positive behaviour and attitudes an emphasis, while being consistent with sanctioning poor behaviour. I modelled the discretionary effort I sought from the students in my lesson preparation. I made every effort to arrive at lessons before the students, calm, organised and well-prepared. I stood at the door to greet students as they entered the room. I made sure the environment was clean, tidy and conducive to learning. I ensured the mood, tone and attitude I projected helped positive learning relationships to form. I reminded myself I was not a victim of my circumstances: I had the ability to change things.

Making a difference

And they did change. I managed to craft classes of students who were ready and willing to learn. The things I have listed here seem obvious now and second nature, but that is because the experience was a necessary part of developing my own sense of agency. Teachers are far more likely to encounter 'swampy ground' than they are 'firm ground', so having a sense of agency positions practitioners in a 'state of readiness' (Garratt, 2005). Every challenge is an opportunity to develop greater capacity and, in turn, agency. I have always believed that great teachers have all the ingredients to be great leaders; the very nature of teaching necessitates the ability to lead.

In his book *Leadership: Plain and Simple*, Steve Radcliffe (2009) outlines the Future–Engage–Deliver model. It is my view that this framework is at the heart of teaching. Teachers conceive a future for their students that does not yet exist. The teacher engages the students, their families and other colleagues to create alignment in achieving the future outcome. The teacher makes use of all the available resources to deliver the desired outcome. Every time this process is completed, the teacher's sense of efficacy and agency is enhanced.

This doesn't apply only to preparing students for examinations. It can be helping students understand a key concept, coaching the Year 7 football team or supporting a student to improve their punctuality: it is the warp and weft of being a teacher. The opportunities are wide and varied, but essential for teachers to grasp their ability to effect change in the lives of others. Great schools are made of 'leaderful teams' (Lingard et al., 2003). The reason players such as Messi and Mbappe are celebrated is ultimately that they have honed their sense of agency to a degree that gives them confidence that they can make a difference. Many teachers would do well to know the value they can and do bring to the young people, schools and communities they serve.

Spark something

Getting things done

Have you ever had a moment when you have been called upon to make a difference? Perhaps to shoot the game-winning shot? Or the final penalty to send your side through? Maybe running the final leg of a 100-metre relay? Although these are all sporting illustrations, they serve as good examples of moments when individual efficacy is key to the overall outcome. Being able to deliver is a superpower. At least it looks that way to observers. The reality is that practice makes proficiency.

Six-time NBA Champion Michael Jordan said 'I've missed more than 9000 shots in my career. I've lost almost 300 games. 26 times, I've been trusted to take the game-winning shot and missed. I've failed over and over and over again in my life. And that is why I succeed' (Nike advert, 1997). In essence, his willingness to keep pushing himself helped him develop his sense of agency.

Confidence comes from competence.

And competence comes from knowledge; namely, knowing how to get things done. The most effective professionals have systems that help them get things done. You might find the following systems useful for completing tasks:

The GTD® method

David Allen (2001) is known for his productivity book *Getting Things Done* (GTD®). He argues that 'Your mind is for having ideas, not holding them'. An integral part of the GTD method is the 'capture' phase, which involves simply capturing everything in your head into a central location. This might seem really basic, but ensure you have a place to record all the commitments, interests and tasks you have. Some prefer a digital tool such as Microsoft® Planner®; others might prefer using the notes app on their smartphone. Personally, my preferred way of capturing information is my A5 weekly planner and notebook. Find what works best for you and stick to it. This will serve as a key feature of your organisational system.

The Eisenhower Matrix

Former US President Dwight D. Eisenhower developed a tool for time management and task prioritisation. To create an Eisenhower Matrix, draw a box with four quadrants on a blank sheet of paper. Label the quadrants as described:

- Top-left quadrant: 'urgent & important'
- Top-right quadrant: 'not urgent & important'
- Bottom-left quadrant: 'urgent & not important'
- Bottom-right quadrant: 'not urgent & not important'.

Krogerus, M. and Tschäppeler, R. (2007)

Now list all the tasks you need to complete in the next week in the respective quadrants. For example, expressing your interest in an internal job role might be designated as 'urgent and important', whereas responding to a new LinkedIn request might be designated 'not urgent and not important'. Once you have captured all the tasks, you should have a sense of where your priorities are.

Here's how to respond to the tasks in each quadrant:

- Urgent & important: Do it now, beginning with the most pressing task.
- Not urgent & important: Schedule a time to do this task.
- Urgent & not important: Consider whether this task could be delegated to somebody else.
- Not urgent & not important: Eliminate this task.

90-minute sprint

The 90-minute sprint (Loehr and Schwartz, 2003) works by blocking out uninterrupted time for deep work on a 'stuck' task. No emails, no social media, no distractions; just focused attention on a particular task.

If the prospect of an uninterrupted 90 minutes seems unrealistic, try breaking the time period into a much smaller chunk. You would be amazed at how much you can do in a thirty-minute block with your total, undivided attention. There are a whole range of time-management techniques designed to help break large assignments into smaller, manageable tasks. Build in rest periods as you conclude one block before moving to the next work session.

CHAPTER 6
BHAG

Great teachers have a vision bigger than themselves

The *why*

One of my all-time favourite films is Ridley Scott's *Gladiator*. Released in 2000, the central character, Maximus Decimus Meridius, serves as an example of qualities that seem rare in contemporary protagonists in literature and film. He is loyal, courageous and noble, but the facet that resonates with me most poignantly is that he lives to achieve an ideal greater than himself. He knows his *why* and, despite the adversity he faces, his vision of what might be provides his drive.

A faithful general under Roman Emperor Marcus Aurelius, Maximus is offered the opportunity to succeed the ailing ruler as regent to restore the Republic. Maximus declines. Meanwhile, the unscrupulous Commodus, Aurelius' son, secretly kills his father, seizes power and requests Maximus' loyalty. Maximus declines. Consequently, Commodus has Maximus arrested and sentenced to death, while mercilessly killing his wife and son. Maximus evades his captors and death, but finds himself wounded and captured by slave traders. He is enslaved.

A key quotation from the film is: 'The general who became a slave. The slave who became a gladiator. The gladiator who defied an emperor. Striking story!' It *is* a striking story, grossing $465.4 million worldwide and amassing five Academy Awards. But what is it that keeps Maximus going? I don't think it is a thirst for power; he declines it. Though he gains it, I don't think it is revenge. I don't think it is a desire for fame and status. He already has it. I think Maximus is driven by a BHAG: a 'Big Hairy Audacious Goal' (Collins, 1994).

The goal

It is a concept developed in Jim Collins' book *Built to Last* (1994). He argues it is a powerful way to stimulate progress because it is clear and compelling, needing little explanation; people get it right away. His research suggested that the best BHAGs require building for the long term as well as creating a relentless sense of urgency. I would propose Maximus' BHAG is to see Rome restored to its former glory. This drives the activity of his professional life, whether leading armies against the Germanic tribes, 'winning the crowd' as a mighty gladiator or defeating the tyrannical rule of Commodus; every iteration of his professional life is connected to the BHAG.

Aside from his life as a soldier, Maximus is a simple and humble man, simply longing to be reunited with his family and harvest his crops. But his BHAG elicits greatness from him and others, even though he does not live to see it realised. His ambition is for others rather than for himself, serving as the foil to the villainous Commodus. Plunged into slavery, he has to start from scratch and learn anew what it is to be a gladiator.

Fullan (2003a) would argue that 'it takes capacity to build capacity'. Maximus' early experiences training as a Roman soldier develop his capacity to be an effective gladiator. And so it is with teachers. Having a BHAG serves as a driving force to grow and develop. Every challenging situation, continuing professional development (CPD) opportunity, new role and responsibility becomes a step closer towards achieving the seemingly impossible goal. My BHAG has been to be the best version of myself as a teacher and I have seen how this has shaped my career, reframing my perspective and experiences.

The growth

As an unqualified teacher, I was given a reduced teaching load, along with a tutor group. I did everything I could to be the best version of myself for my classes, reading educational research and literature, observing experienced colleagues, attending internal and external CPD, reading widely to develop my subject knowledge. I worked closely with the year leader, Rhiannon Dillon, who became a dear friend and mentor, to understand how to be an effective tutor, to liaise with parents, to challenge and support students and to motivate and manage a team of teachers.

I was appointed to my first teaching and learning opportunity in my newly qualified teacher (NQT) year, working as the whole-school literacy co-ordinator. I worked with senior and middle leaders to develop a whole-school strategy. I delivered assemblies to students and organised 'Drop Everything and Read' events to help foster a love of reading. I worked with BookTrust to facilitate every Year 7 joining the school to receive a free book of their choice. I worked with parents and carers to encourage them to dedicate time at home to reading together with their children.

As an NQT+1, I was appointed as the Head of Year 7. I gained insights into transition, admissions and marketing. I worked with families to support their children in developing high expectations and standards. I supported the most vulnerable learners in the cohort, working with the SEND team, educational welfare officer, the virtual school and foster carers. I worked with external agencies to tackle bullying, anti-social behaviour and low-level crime, as well as key members of the governing body.

After my first three years as a qualified teacher, I had garnered experience and expertise that caused me to grow exponentially, both personally and professionally. Of course, I made a myriad of mistakes! But I also made lots of marginal gains. I did not realise it at the time, but my BHAG to be the best version of myself necessitated that I employ a growth mindset. In *Mindset*, Dweck (2012) argues that growth-minded leaders:

> ... start with a belief in human potential and development – both their own and other people's. Instead of using the company as a vehicle for their greatness, they use it as an engine of growth – for themselves, the employees, and the company as a whole.

I saw that the school itself was an engine of growth. As I was given opportunities to excel, this in turn would allow others to excel. It is hard to coast or stagnate when you are driven by a goal that creates relentless urgency. You become like the Tardis from the BBC fiction *Doctor Who*, because you are bigger on the inside than the outside. By design, a BHAG creates movement. If fear paralyses and forces us to stay put, a BHAG forces us to move. Personally, my BHAG has pushed me to take on roles and responsibilities that always felt bigger than me. To be the very best version of myself I can be in any given situation? That's a big ask. It's audacious. It takes audacity to say you want to be the best, especially when there is no evidence to corroborate this. But anybody who has ever done anything worthy of note has this audacity.

Taking action

It will offend people who cannot see it. It might rub people up the wrong way. If you walk into your department and say 'I want every student in my class to secure a grade 4 / 5 / 6 / 7 / 8 / 9' (delete as appropriate), you will possibly be met with raised eyebrows, objections, sympathetic smiles or a dose of 'realism'. My fear is that often the reason why our young people fail to reach their potential is not that we aim high and miss it, but rather that we aim low and achieve it.

Such a goal would create urgency and action. You would need to ensure, as a teacher, you have the subject knowledge and pedagogical skill to deliver the respective teaching. Your students would need to be clear on the goal, and motivated to employ the necessary work ethic, attitude, knowledge, skill and understanding. The families of those young people would need to provide additional support to ensure excellent attendance, punctuality and behaviour; a suitable learning environment at home; along with the necessary resources and clear structures, routines and emotional support. All this because you walked in with a BHAG.

Senge (2006) argues that the gap between our vision (or the BHAG we seek to achieve) and our current reality generates a creative tension that, like a rubber band, either pulls the vision to reality or the reality to the vision. Elsewhere, Senge writes 'an organisation's commitment to and capacity for learning can be no greater than that of its members'. What is your BHAG? What could happen if you had a clearly articulated BHAG? For you personally? Professionally? Your department? Your school? The young people? The wider community?

It takes audacity to have a future vision that does not align with the current reality; but the audacity to believe things can be better is the ultimate outworking of teaching like your heart is on fire.

Spark something

BHAG

I think that anything ever done in history that is worthy of note was underpinned and / or driven by a Big Hairy Audacious Goal. Think of some feat of human tenacity, such as Sir Roger Bannister being the first man to run a mile in under four minutes. He set himself a BHAG. He achieved it on 6 May 1954. Just 46 days later, his record was broken by a rival. Bannister's BHAG pushed him and others to be better versions of themselves.

Teachers should be among some of the most audacious of people. Our ambition for our young people, our schools and the communities we serve should be self-evident. Every school I have ever worked in has always had challenges. Of course every school has challenges, but by 'challenges' I mean the wicked problems that are not easy to fix: high levels of social deprivation, negative attitudes towards schools and education by both students and parents, poor and anti-social behaviour – the list goes on. But I have always worked with inspiring leaders who held high hopes for the young people, the school and the wider community.

It's audacious to hold a vision of what the future could be in spite of the overwhelm of current present realities. Our schools need leaders at every level committed to rallying others to a better future. And that's why a BHAG is so important. It is a clear and compelling goal, and I want to help you create your own. If you were to realise your potential fully, what might that look like for your students? Some steps to help you reverse-engineer your BHAG follow:

1. **Build the BHAG**

   - Write it in a single, bold sentence.

   - Make it specific, measurable and time-bound (for example 'By 2028, 80% of my students will achieve grade 5+ in English.').

   - Ensure it's inspiring and just beyond current reach.

2. **Mark the milestones**

   - Break the long-term BHAG into big staging posts (for example termly or half-termly outcomes).

   - Ask yourself: 'What must be true by the end of Term 1, Term 2, Term 3 for us to reach the BHAG?'

3. **List the key levers**

   - Select the two to three most powerful drivers of change.

   - Ask: 'If we did only a few things exceptionally well, which would make the biggest difference?'

4. **State the strategy**

   - Turn each lever into a strategic strand (first-quality teaching, independent practice).

   - Under each strand, note two to three key initiatives.

5. **Break it down into bite-size actions**

   - For each initiative, set termly or half-termly deliverables.

   - Ask: 'What should be visible within 90 days if we're on track?'

6. **Allocate ownership and accountability**

   - Make it clear who is responsible for each lever and milestone.

   - Build in reporting structures (for example check-ins and reviews).

7. **Stress-test the plan**

   - Imagine obstacles (for example student absence, lack of progress).

   - Ask: 'If we got stuck here, what's Plan B?'

8. **Keep beating the BHAG drum**

   - Revisit it in every lesson, parent meeting and line-management meeting.

   - Use it as the filter for decision-making: 'Does this move us closer to the BHAG?'

PART 3
CULTURE

CHAPTER 7
BE THE CHANGE

Great teachers contribute to the culture

When life flows smoothly

As a media studies teacher, I keep a collection of notable adverts that help to explore wider societal issues. One of my favourites is 'Cog', launched by Honda® in 2003 to promote the seventh-generation Accord line of cars. It shows several disassembled parts in real time create a domino effect, culminating in the big reveal of the new car. (Have a look for it online. It's definitely worth a watch if you have never seen it.)

It illustrates the synchronicity of each component working together to create the final outcome. The message is that we appreciate it when life flows smoothly with no hiccups, but the commercial took 100 takes to film over four days, so there is a contrast between the message and the hard work that went into the advert.

We do appreciate it when life flows smoothly, but it rarely does *just* work out like that. Most things of value and worth require a great deal of attention and care, like the proverbial swan that paddles furiously beneath the water, yet appears to glide with ease. The same is true of an excellent organisational culture. It takes work. Every component has to work together to create the desired outcome.

Be the light

We all contribute to the culture we exist in. If I may, I would like to borrow imagery from the Christian faith. Christ taught his disciples that his followers are supposed to be salt and light in the world. Think about how salt has the ability to transform a meal. In the ancient Middle East, salt would both preserve food and enhance flavour. It seeks no permission and makes no apology; just its mere presence brings about change. Likewise, light has the power to permeate darkness. There is no ambiguity. Light is, well, light. It is useful. It is helpful. In a darkened room, light is unmistakable. Neither salt nor light requires an external force, but is itself the catalyst that exerts influence on whatever it is applied to. And they do not need to exist in huge quantities to be effective.

A great teacher is the same. This is not to set an impossible standard. Nobody is saying that teachers must be automatons with smiles plastered on their faces at all times, but every teacher actively adds to (or subtracts from) the culture. For instance, consider the old teaching adage, 'don't smile until Christmas'. I get it. I understand why this advice has become dogma for some. But what message does it communicate to the young people we serve about how we feel about the job, about them and about the importance of education? It belies an attitude of disdain at the very least; very often to young people who lack positive role models in other areas of their lives.

In his book *Good to Great*, Jim Collins writes 'If you have the right people on the bus, the problem of how to motivate and manage people largely goes away. The right people don't need to be tightly managed or fired up; they will be self-motivated by the inner drive to produce the best results and to be part of creating something great'. While I recognise the importance of teacher recruitment, I believe it is possible to become the right person. It begins with a recognition of your influence and how you contribute to the culture; a desire to achieve something great: a BHAG.

Tipping point

That's how you reach a tipping point – the hinge point when things change. Gladwell (2000) contends that 'epidemics are a function of the people who transmit infectious agents, the infectious agent itself, and the environment in which the infectious agent is operating'. Great schools are filled with adults infected with a relentless optimism, which spreads to the young people they serve and beyond. Having lived through a global pandemic, we have some experience of how quickly and easily a virus can be transmitted. In Christopher Nolan's 2010 film *Inception*, the main protagonist states: 'an idea is like a virus, resilient, highly contagious. The smallest seed of an idea can grow. It can grow to define or destroy you'. If we were to record the average teacher, day in and day out, every lesson, interaction, conversation, gesture, and so on, like Channel 4's *Educating Yorkshire* documentary, what would we derive about their ideas on education?

One of my most poignant lessons as a teacher took place in my first teaching post. I had a challenging class of Year 8 boys who I found really difficult to teach. I used to dread this class. I felt like the students would actively seek opportunities to wreck my lesson. It was the same disruptive behaviour they demonstrated in other parts of the school and they were renowned for being disengaged and disaffected. I would speak to other colleagues who had the same experience and I was conscious of the danger that our professional conversations were simply becoming an echo chamber of negativity.

I started to talk up my class to others. I told my class that I believed they would become my favourite class to teach by the end of the academic year. I would tell them I was looking forward to teaching them. I didn't realise it at the time, but I was shaping their expectations of themselves. I planted a resilient, highly contagious idea in both their minds and my own. Their behaviour slowly began to improve and the students began to make progress. Later that academic year, I was inspected by the lead inspector (HMI) during an Ofsted inspection, who stated 'in an outstanding Year 8 lesson, the teacher's high expectations, allied to great enthusiasm and skill, enabled exceptionally low attainers to confidently express views about the social and moral consequences of their actions'. They did become my favourite class.

My point is less about an Ofsted grade but, to highlight, I was able to exert my influence on a group of disengaged, disaffected, disillusioned but impressionable young people. They came to my lesson believing they were incapable of learning and making progress in English. And when I experienced their poor behaviour, I was infected with the same idea. The epiphany came when I changed the idea. Gruenert and Whitaker (2017) argue that culture serves as the 'guiding beliefs and values, a social indoctrination of unwritten rules learnt to fit into a particular group, the way we do things around here, software for the mind, the default mode of behaviour and so on'. How many of our young people (and their teachers) need an upgrade to their operating system?

Vote for change

It was within my power to be the change I hoped to see. And I wasn't lying to that Year 8 class. I just reframed how I looked at them – an *appreciative inquiry* of the issues I faced. In his book *Atomic Habits*, James Clear writes 'every action you take is a vote for the type of person you wish to become. No single instance will transform your beliefs, but as the votes build up, so does the evidence of your new identity ... small habits can make a meaningful difference by providing evidence of a new identity'. If this is true, it follows that every statement I made to and about my class was a vote for the type of class I hoped they would become. My beliefs influenced my actions; my actions shaped the beliefs of the young people I taught.

Before I ever worked at one of my favourite schools in my career to date, I remember the then headteacher giving me a tour and observing him pick up the occasional pieces of litter we came across as we walked around the school.

With every bit of paper or lost pen lid, he implicitly communicated that the school environment was important and what took place there was important and the people who worked there were important. I watched his senior team do the same. They modelled to everyone in the building that we were all stewards of our learning environment. We were all contributing to the culture, always. Every action is a vote for the school we want to work in.

Outsiders might muse to themselves, how lovely it is when life flows smoothly and all the cogs and moving parts spin with ease and things just work. But things don't *just* work. They are the outcome of deliberate, thoughtful action. Our young people will not *just* attend school regularly, or demonstrate excellent behaviour, or make significant progress. Our classrooms will not *just* be vibrant learning environments, our schools will not *just* be great places to work, flourish and thrive; not unless we are infected with the relentless optimism that it takes to transform a cohort, a school community or a life.

Spark something

Be the change

Culture eats strategy for breakfast.

David Campbell et al., 2011

Peter Drucker was so right. It doesn't matter how clear our strategy is; it will not land impactfully if the organisational culture is not right. All of us as individuals bring our own values, beliefs and behaviours that coalesce into what we call 'culture'. If the organisational culture is tended to with care and attention, it can be a powerful driver: that feeling of 'that's just how we do things round here'. It's the feeling we get when we visit an excellent restaurant or stay in an exquisite hotel. We get the impression that every little detail has been considered and curated to communicate the brand: the gut feeling a consumer has about an organisation. And it's not always *what* is done, but *how* it's done.

It's the reason why the best organisations take recruitment (and retention) so seriously, because ultimately it is the people in the organisation who either enhance or erode the culture. People won't always remember what you say, but they remember how you made them feel. Your overall impression of an organisation can be shaped by how the receptionist greeted you or how attentive the waiter was or how clean the Uber® driver's vehicle was. All organisations rely on the individuals that comprise it to communicate the culture.

In your organisation, how do you make your primary stakeholders – your young people – feel? It's in the little things. In Dickens' *A Christmas Carol*, Scrooge reminisces on his experience of his former employer Fezziwig, saying 'He has the power to render us happy or unhappy; to make our service light or burdensome: a pleasure or a toil. Say that his power lies in words and looks; in things so slight and insignificant that it is impossible to add and count 'em up – what then? The happiness he gives, is quite as great, as if it cost a fortune'.

Even the stingy, hardened Ebenezer Scrooge could recognise how culture is created and maintained. Our power as teachers can render our students happy or unhappy, their experience light or burdensome, a pleasure or a toil. And where does our power lie? In words and looks and things so slight and insignificant. Beyond the basics of clear routines and structures, teachers have a great deal of influence on the experience of their young people.

I have worked with colleagues in a Science Department who always wear colourful bowties on Fridays. I worked with a head of modern foreign languages who would issue his students a coloured foldback clip for excellent work in class. The children would wear them on their blazer as a badge of honour. I worked with a teacher who would bake for her GCSE classes at the end of the academic year as a reward. In these slight and insignificant ways, these colleagues cultivated positive working relationships with their students. As the adults in the building, we make the weather. The following suggestions indicate how you might contribute to the culture of your school.

Conduct a corridor culture audit

Take the opportunity one break time intentionally to observe and notice the tone, habits and energy of your school culture. What do you notice? Is there anything you could do to enhance it? Perhaps strike up a conversation with a child standing without companions? Maybe there's an opportunity to model picking up litter and putting it in a bin? Channel the boisterous energy of a group of students into a productive and constructive conversation about their interests?

Lead by micro-example

Choose one daily habit to model relentlessly. Perhaps it might be to model punctuality and arrive earlier than normal to your classroom to allow you to greet every student on arrival. Maybe it might be ensuring that you give a sincere, thoughtful greeting to everyone you meet in the morning. You could have a big focus on praising excellent uniform and positively challenging instances of poor uniform.

Keep a culture contribution log

While we recognise that the things that contribute to culture can be slight and insignificant, the impact can add up to what seems a great fortune. For one week, at the end of each day, write down one small way you contributed positively to the school culture. By the end of the week, you will have codified a range of actions that helped to shape the culture. You might even get some student voice to help establish the impact of your contributions. Where attention goes, energy flows; having a deliberate focus on how you are shaping the culture will help you continue to be intentional in your contributions.

CHAPTER 8
CHEERS

Great teachers create a sense of belonging

'Where Everybody Knows Your Name'

As a child growing up in the 90s, I didn't really get all of the humour from the 1980s sitcom *Cheers*. I was too young to understand all the subtleties and nuances of the adult experience. But I did understand the theme song 'Where Everybody Knows Your Name'. (Have a look online for the song and lyrics. It's definitely worth a listen if you have never heard it.)

I recognise the theme song is about the fictional patrons of a Boston bar, but there is something powerful about feeling seen, feeling valued, feeling known, going somewhere everybody knows your name. It is my view that schools should give students that same feeling of safety and security. Students should enjoy their education, not endure it. Many young people do endure it, experiencing education as pariahs for any number of reasons. It is in the power of teachers to make schools a place where students feel like they belong; that they are part of something. Bush and Middlewood (2005) argue that organisational culture is made up of four major features:

1. Values and beliefs
2. Shared norms and meanings
3. Rituals and ceremonies (symbols)
4. Heroes and heroines.

These factors shape the organisational culture of our classrooms, school corridors and wider school community. They serve as the foundation for crafting an environment that breeds a sense of belonging. This, however, is not about creating an environment that mollycoddles students. For the most disadvantaged students, that is the worst thing we could do. Expectation shapes performance. There is no advantage in belonging to an organisation with low expectations, low standards and low aspirations. Bennett (2017) writes:

The vision for what constitutes acceptable and desirable behaviour should be clearly communicated to all members of staff and students. Students must be made constantly aware of the expectations required of them. Expectations must be not only high, but demonstrated repeatedly, and consistently.

High standards and high expectations of our young people communicate safety and trust because our practices are consistent and there is clarity about what the culture rewards and sanctions. When we belong, we know what to expect, we know where we fit and the role we play. We are free of the anxiety that can be induced by uncertainty and ambiguity. The very nature of learning requires a level of vulnerability students and staff are unwilling to display if they feel psychologically unsafe. You want to go where everybody knows your name, a place where you are valued as an individual, a place where you can be vulnerable.

School must be that place where young people are safe to be vulnerable as they learn, grow and develop into adults, cocooned and sheltered from what can be a cold and dark world, transformed into active citizens that can contribute to society. What happens inside the Black Box of our classrooms and schools is what makes the difference to young people, and often leads to those frisson moments you see in teacher-recruitment adverts. I have had several of those moments throughout my career, but the one that has stuck with me throughout my time as a teacher and school leader took place in that challenging school in South London.

Bringing learning to life

It was 2012 and I was teaching *Of Mice and Men* to my Year 10 English class. The class comprised students with a range of learning needs, as well as a number of students with English as an additional language. One student's first language was Polish and she was still in the early stages of language acquisition. We were reading the final chapter of the book. I would read aloud to the class, replete with questionable American accents and sound effects, as the class followed along in their copies. I read the climactic scene, speaking as both characters and ending with a sound effect of a booming gunshot. As I surveyed the room, I saw the student in floods of tears.

At first I was confused as to why she was crying. I wondered if the text had triggered some trauma I was unaware of. I discreetly gestured to ask her if she was OK and she nodded and smiled. Nobody laughed or drew attention to her unexpected outpouring of emotion. She looked a little embarrassed and continued with her work. As I reflected, it dawned on me that perhaps her tears were a direct response to what we had read. I hadn't anticipated such a response. I had not considered that literature could have such a powerful impact on my students. I had underestimated how a sense of belonging and safety in the classroom could elicit such vulnerability.

A decade or so later, I got the opportunity to ask the student whether she remembered that moment. She did and she told me:

The reason I cried was that the ending of the book was very sad: two best friends who were very close to each other. One of them had to make a difficult decision and kill the other, so he didn't suffer. This was very moving in my opinion and caused me to cry. The way you read the book with so much passion had an impact on it too. If you had just read the book in a kind of neutral tone, I don't think it would have affected me in that way as much. In my opinion, as a teacher you always taught very well and you had such a great impact on all the students. You were passionate and enthusiastic each lesson and you delivered a message to students in an engaging way.

When I read that, it humbled me. It highlighted what a powerful position we are placed in as teachers. In that moment, the English lesson was all that mattered. The literature was all that mattered. Lennie and George were all that mattered. She learned that literature has the power to move us deeply. She demonstrated empathy and compassion. She saw the power of communication and how words on a page can stir our hearts and minds. In that lesson, she had an experience that would reverberate through her memories and shape her worldview. I was not expecting that response when I assumed the roles of George and Lennie. In that moment, I was simply teaching with my heart on fire.

It wasn't really about me. It was about the learning. The class may have felt disconnected from the complexities of the Great Depression in 1930s America, but they felt connected to me and each other and were therefore prepared to take a foray into the unfamiliar text. From the familiar to the unfamiliar, great leaders rally people to a better future.

MediaManiacs

It is why, later in my career when I became head of media studies in a different setting, I developed the brand identity MediaManiacs for students studying GCSE and A-level media. I wanted the young people to belong to a subculture within the wider school community. I got T-shirts printed that student ambassadors wore at open evenings and special events. I introduced an Oscars-style award ceremony, replete with red carpets and the associated glitz and glamour, to showcase student work to students and their families at the end of the academic year.

It was an opportunity to celebrate explicitly the values of creativity and craftsmanship; our belief that we should put beauty into the world. We got to enjoy the fruits of our labours, reflecting on the shared experiences of planning, researching, producing, editing and presenting a media product. It was a ritual to commend the heroes and heroines of our mini community, highlighting those who exemplified best the values of a MediaManiac. I was able to create special memories for the young people in my charge. It was in my gift to give them a sense of belonging, which in turn built trust and commitment; necessary ingredients for high-performing teams.

Slight and insignificant means

Let's revisit Ebenezer Scrooge reflecting on his experience as an apprentice under his former employer, Fezziwig: 'He has the power to render us happy or unhappy; to make our service light or burdensome: a pleasure or a toil. Say that his power lies in words and looks; in things so slight and insignificant that it is impossible to add and count 'em up – what then? The happiness he gives, is quite as great, as if it cost a fortune' (Dickens, 1843). Teachers shape the future through a myriad of seemingly 'slight and insignificant' means. Our actions and words make or break the experience of education our young people encounter. Life can be hard, the world cold, and times tough; as our young people make their way through the world, school can and should be a place where somebody knows their name.

Spark something

Cheers

'A person's name is to that person, the sweetest and most important sound in any language'. This quotation was popularised by Dale Carnegie, author of *How to Win Friends and Influence People*. He rightly identified the significance of our names. Our names are important because they are a fundamental part of our identity, our background, our culture, our heritage. When you use somebody's name, you affirm and recognise their personal history.

Using a person's name is a simple and effective way to build connections in both professional and personal relationships. It's why we still write greetings cards to our Dear Sam or Dear Ade. Nicknames, too, have special significance because they carry shared knowledge and meaning. Furthermore, hearing your name can make you feel seen, appreciated and valued as an individual, distinct from the crowd. You are recognised as a human being worthy of dignity and respect.

With all the push and pull factors young people face beyond school, our objective is to create a learning environment that helps everyone feel they belong. Schools should be one place in society where a child can feel known and seen and safe, where the adults they interact with are pleased they came. The difference between the Bull and Finch Pub in *Cheers* and our schools is that, rather than creating belonging by drowning sorrows in the present, we create belonging with the intentional purpose of helping our students build opportunities for their futures.

The suggestions that follow are ways you can build belonging in your classroom and beyond:

Warm welcomes

Each lesson, stand at your door and give a personal greeting to each of your students. It helps set the tone, and allows you to gauge your students' readiness for learning.

Two-minute check-in

As appropriate, spend two minutes at the start of the week in conversation with a student you don't usually chat with. Ask about their weekend, interests or feelings about what they have been learning. It helps students understand how to engage in polite and cordial small talk, as well as giving you an opportunity to gain greater awareness about your class.

Class playlist

This might be an activity for a class with which you have built good rapport. Invite students to suggest songs that represent them, lift their mood or help them to study. You could play snippets on special occasions or key moments during the year.

Cultural calendar

Consider the makeup of your class and mark any key cultural, religious or community events represented in your classroom. It provides an opportunity to celebrate meaningful moments. Even a brief acknowledgment signals value.

Acknowledge absence

When a student is absent, acknowledge their absence and, where appropriate, let them know they were missed. It is an opportunity to reiterate their contribution to the class and encourage their attendance.

Classroom charter

This is a helpful activity for new classes or the start of a new academic term or year. Outline your expectations and co-create an agreement of how students will treat each other. If appropriate, display it and revisit it regularly across the term.

Photo collage

As appropriate, capture photos of class life (with consent) and create a digital collage to show shared identity. This can be particularly impactful for classes in the final year of their academic careers.

Be vulnerable

As appropriate, share something about yourself (an ambition, a favourite song, a family tradition). By modelling openness, students have a greater willingness to reciprocate.

CHAPTER 9
A WORD TO LEADERS

Great school leaders nurture great teachers

Nobody comes to work to do a bad job

I sincerely believe this is true in most cases, so when things are going wrong it's necessary to unpick what is happening. It is part and parcel of being a leader. Great leaders look after their people. Good people are the biggest asset to any organisation, especially schools. Therefore, it is incumbent on leaders to take care of the adults who take care of the children in our schools.

The primary and perhaps most critical way that leaders can nurture great teachers is by looking for the right character. Bush and Middlewood (2013) suggest that leaders can shape or change culture 'through the appointment of other staff who have the same values and beliefs, leading to cultural consonance ... the staff selection process provides an opportunity to set out the values of the school'. Do they possess the self-awareness to know their motives for teaching? What do they believe about intelligence? What do they believe about young people? The recruitment process is critical for developing excellent teachers. They must possess raw materials that great leaders and schools are able to hone, refine and enhance. Does your school-recruitment process in its current form allow you to identify the raw talent great teachers possess?

Great leaders have a (often unwritten) framework that serves as a competency model, which helps to recruit people with similar competencies or the potential to develop these assets (Goleman et al., 2002; Keating and Heslin, 2015). How do you spot a potentially great teacher during the recruitment process through aspects such as application forms, school tours and interview questions? The purpose of these instruments should be to elicit cues about intrinsic qualities such as character and commitment. The coalescence of staff beliefs into shared values means that 'over time, the culture of the school will shift in the direction sought by the principal' (Bush and Middlewood, 2013).

Recruitment is the first gateway to developing excellent teachers. If someone doesn't have a desire to be excellent, I do not think they can be coerced into it. Fullan (2003a) argues that 'providing professional autonomy to groups of teachers who don't have the commitment ... and moral purpose will do no more than squander resources'. Discerning the character of colleagues is essential for knowing how best to support them – that is the role of the leader. It's too easy to write off somebody whose performance is not where it needs to be. Nobody comes to work to do a bad job.

Recruitment and retention

Too often, teachers are simply used like an expendable resource. The stories of teachers burning out and / or leaving the profession are commonplace. Bottery (2012) rightly contends that educational leaders and schools must reject attempts to 'extract all available work, every last drop of effort, in order to rack up record results in a more efficient manner'. Within education, teacher motivation is a rich, natural resource that must be sustainably sourced, otherwise the overuse and depletion of this resource will lead to the decline in the quality of systems overall.

The emphasis for successive governments has been recruitment when there should also have been a sharp focus on retention. Great schools recognise this and invest time and energy into making their schools great places to work despite the external pressures they face. Schools can and should be a great place to work for everyone, regardless of which stage of their career they are in. We all need different things at different points of our careers and professional development to be our best.

Hargreaves and Fullan (2012a) helpfully articulate how our relationships with work change during our careers:

- **Early career:** Hargreaves and Fullan (2012a) argue that, at the start of our teaching careers, we have higher levels of commitment. Imagine the brand-new teacher eager to change the lives of young people; full of energy and enthusiasm, but lacking the necessary experience and expertise to have an effective impact.

- **Mid-career:** They argue that, as we progress in our careers, we develop the expertise and experience that comes with being at the chalkface. We earn our stripes as practitioners and can match high levels of capability with high levels of commitment.

- **Late career:** Their argument concludes that, as we reach the latter stages of our careers, the priorities of our lives change significantly, and we begin to redirect our energies to other areas of our lives. These colleagues retain a wealth of experience and knowledge, yet prefer to invest their lives in other personal commitments rather than their professional careers.

Without making sweeping generalisations, this does accurately capture the professional life of a teacher, although it is not unique to teaching. And at every point, teachers should be supported to do their best work.

Performance and behaviours

In his book *Leadership Matters*, Buck (2017) outlines the various performance and behaviours leaders can experience in their teams. Every teacher falls into one of these categories at every phase of their career. Regardless of whether a colleague is in the early, middle or later stages of their career, I would argue that everyone has the potential to be a great teacher, except the colleague who is not committed to their growth. Their influence needs to be removed or neutralised because of the insidious effect it has on the wider culture. An organisation's commitment to and capacity for learning can be no greater than that of its members (Senge, 2006). If a teacher is not willing to grow, they have a limiting effect on the rest of the organisation.

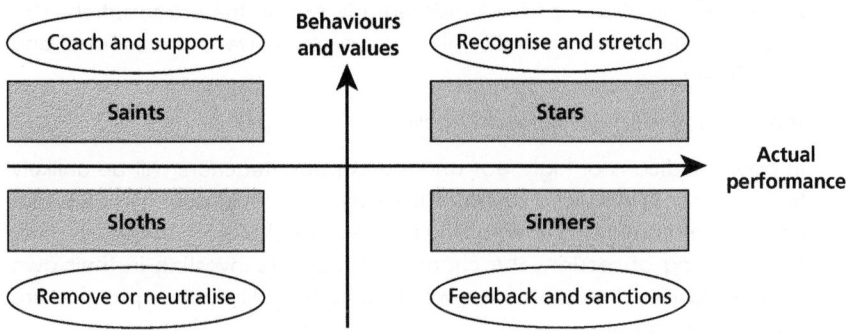

Performance and behaviours (Buck, 2017)

It is not the leader's role to put into a teacher the desire to be excellent. Rather, Fullan (2003b) argues that the leader's role is to change the context through introducing new elements into the situation that influence behaviour for the better; if you change the situation, you can change how people behave in the short and long term. 'If you do not also focus on changing the culture and working conditions of schools ... good teachers will not stay long – or come in the first place' (Fullan, 2003b).

Growth environments

Leaders are charged with the task of creating environments where excellent teachers want to come, want to stay and have the opportunity to grow. If you create a safe space for your people to flourish, they will. Senge (2006) contends 'there is nothing more important to an individual committed to his or her own growth than a supportive environment'. It seems incongruous to expect a workforce to maintain a growth mindset about the young people they work with, while maintaining a fixed mindset about the capacity of the workforce to grow. We all need different things at different points of our careers and our professional development.

Nobody is born a great teacher. They are crafted and forged by their environments. It is possible for great teachers to emerge from toxic cultures and working environments; it's just more difficult and more painful and unnecessary. Leithwood et al. (2006) note 'leadership serves as a catalyst for unleashing the potential capacities that already exist in the organisation'. This happens best when the organisational culture is conducive to professional and personal growth.

Hargreaves and Fullan (2012a) wisely posit:

> In poor conditions of high fear and low support, teachers will be unlikely to invest in each other or even in themselves. In confident climates that encourage growth and even a little risk because they provide an essential underpinning of security, the chances of teachers investing in their own development and reaping the rewards of high quality in their practice are considerably greater.

It is the role of the leader to give constant attention to the organisational culture, tending to it like a gardener, encouraging growth and removing the weeds that damage a healthy ecosystem. One way to encourage growth is by challenging the 'tendency to target only the most proven candidates by instead giving serious consideration to those candidates whose performance capability might be most developed by assuming a challenging new role for which they do not yet have all the required competencies' (Keating and Heslin, 2015). This is often how great teachers are formed; by providing space, a role or responsibility for committed individuals to grow into – the audacious fill that void as they expand their capacity.

Keating and Heslin (2015) argue that 'cynicism about the utility of high effort ... as well as fear about one's self-image, status, and career consequence of failing' are hallmarks of an organisational culture with diminished psychological safety. Build an environment where great teachers are encouraged to grow and take risks and you develop a culture of excellence. It takes audacity to be great, but daring to be excellent is not so high a risk if the culture is right.

Animal Farm

In George Orwell's *Animal Farm* (1945), Boxer is described as being able to do the work of three horses, making him an invaluable asset to Animal Farm:

Boxer was the admiration of everybody ... always at the spot where the work was hardest ... His answer to every problem, every setback, was 'I will work harder!' – which he had adopted as his personal motto. But everyone worked according to his capacity.

Everybody has encountered a Boxer; a highly motivated individual who seems to flourish in the face of challenges. It seems that his motivation is predicated on his belief that he possesses the potential to develop his abilities through the exertion of effort. Boxer exhibits the type of mindset and motivation that most, if not all, organisations crave in their employees (Clark, 2012). It's definitely the mindset of a great teacher.

But, like Boxer, there are many great teachers being sent to the 'knacker's' because many schools are 'greedy organisations' (Gronn, 2003 cited in Bottery, 2012) that exploit the pursuit of excellence rather than nurture it. 'Leaders have the main responsibility for generating and sustaining culture' (Bush and Middlewood, 2013). If we want excellent teachers in our schools, then we must be excellent leaders: great leaders nurture great teachers.

Spark something

A word to leaders

Nobody comes to work to do a bad job. If we always begin with this maxim, it informs our leadership, helping us to be curious, empathetic and supportive. Leaders make the weather. They create the climate (how it feels), which in turn shapes the culture (what we do). When you are in a position of leadership, it is easy to lose track of how it feels for everybody else.

This is why gathering feedback is so critical. Feedback is a gift. It comes in different shapes and sizes, shades and hues. A large part of a leadership team's job is to collate all the intel and bits of data to allow for synthesis; a triangulation of data to form an evidence base. If all the evidence points to a healthy, thriving organisational culture and climate, well done: you are doing lots of things really well.

The reality is that this is often not the case for a myriad of reasons. Schools are complex places, as are the people who work in them. There is no silver bullet and I won't attempt to provide one here. However, I do want to offer some examples of excellent practice I have observed in great leaders I have worked with that may be of help.

Joy audit

Ask colleagues which part of their job brings them the most joy, and explore how you can help them do more of it. Effective professional development reviews should incorporate elements of this to allow staff to connect their work with purpose.

Fast feedback

Give colleagues one piece of specific, positive feedback this week without any delay, hesitation or caveats. Be quick to praise when people are doing the right thing.

Shield your team

Shield your team from one unnecessary initiative or task this month. Be clear on your rationale and let your colleagues feel your care and protection.

Gratitude walk

Complete a quick gratitude walk through the school once a week, stopping to thank colleagues for something specific you've noticed them doing.

Cover the duty

As appropriate, take over a duty or cover slot once a term for a colleague so they get some unexpected breathing space.

Open door

Block out time in a week when any colleague can drop in for conversation, not complaints. This is about being accessible to colleagues who may not otherwise have the opportunity to speak to you.

Resources boost

As appropriate, ask each department: 'What's one resource that would make your work easier?' Explore different ways of providing the resource to the respective team.

Celebrate small wins

During weekly bulletins or briefings, spotlight a small win achieved by a staff member, department or year group.

Wellbeing check-in

Make a point to check in personally with three colleagues per week (especially quieter or overlooked colleagues). Ask, 'How are you, really?' Effective line management should provide space for this, but this activity provides greater opportunity for dialogue.

Exit interviews for staying staff

Exit interviews are a helpful tool for gathering insights from colleagues leaving the organisation. However, once a year, interview staff members intending to stay and ask: 'What keeps you here? What would make you leave?' Use these insights to improve the culture and climate before people walk out.

The leadership culture must be a positive one for these activities to have the desired effect.

CONCLUSION

And so we have arrived at the end of the book. You can remove the bookmark, or unfold the page corner, place it on your bookshelf, share it with a friend, leave it in the staff room or give it as a gift to a newbie to the profession like Georgina did for me. We're done. It's like when teachers wipe their whiteboards clean (when I first started teaching, I had a rolling chalkboard, which was quite the flex in the late 00s!); they erase the messy working-out scrawled on the board that facilitated the learning, trusting that the learning will remain. I hope that my scrawl on these pages hasn't been too messy, but rather that it has brought clarity:

Clarity about the type of character we need to be great teachers. Clarity about the importance of continually increasing our capacity. Clarity about the type of cultures that create and retain and sustain great teachers. I hope that something you have read here has sparked something in you and that the learning will remain beyond our time together. Why? Our young people need highly skilled, highly motivated teachers to shape the trajectories of their lives. Remember: *the right people don't need to be tightly managed or fired up; they will be self-motivated by the inner drive to produce the best results and to be part of creating something great.* In the context of education, teaching like your heart is on fire describes the inner drive to produce the best results in other people's lives: to shape the future.

You are part of something great. You belong to a pantheon of educators through the ages, who have dedicated their lives to public service. You make the difference. Go, therefore, and teach like your heart is on fire.

REFERENCES

Allen, D. (2001) *Getting Things Done: The Art of Stress-Free Productivity*. New York: Viking.

Bennett, T. (2017) 'Tom Bennett Independent Review of Behaviour in Schools: Creating a culture: how school leaders can optimise behaviour'. London: Department for Education. Available at: https://assets.publishing.service.gov.uk/government/uploads/system/uploads/attachment_data/file/602487/Tom_Bennett_Independent_Review_of_Behaviour_in_Schools.pdf (Accessed: 1 November 2025)

Bottery, M. (2012) 'Leadership, the Logic of Sufficiency and the Sustainability of Education' in *Educational Management Administration & Leadership*, 40(4), pp.449–463.

Buck, A. (2017) *Leadership Matters: How Leaders at All Levels Can Create Great Schools*. Cambridge: John Catt Educational.

Bush, T. and Middlewood, D. (2005) *Leading and Managing People in Education*. London: SAGE.

Bush, T. and Middlewood, D. (2013) 'Organizational cultures' in *Leading and Managing People in Education* (3rd edn). London: Sage, pp.53–65.

Campbell, A., McNamara, O. and Gilroy, P. (2003) 'Professional Identity: Who am I?' in *Practitioner Research and Professional Development in Education*. London: Paul Chapman, pp.28–48.

Carnegie, D. (1936) *How to Win Friends and Influence People*. New York: Simon & Schuster.

Charlesworth, R. (2001) *The Coach: Managing for Success*. Australia: Macmillan Australia.

Clark, T. (2012) 'Engagement Mindset' in *Leadership excellence*, 29(8), p.15.

Clear, J. (2018) *Atomic Habits: Tiny Changes, Remarkable Results*. New York: Avery.

Collins, J. (2001) *Good to Great: Why Some Companies Make the Leap... and Others Don't*. London: Random House Business.

Collins, J. and Porras, J.I. (1994) *Built to Last: Successful Habits of Visionary Companies*. New York: HarperBusiness.

Czubaj, C.A. (1996) 'Maintaining teacher motivation' in *Education*, 116(3), pp.372–379.

Dahl, R. (1988) *Matilda*. London: Jonathan Cape.

Day, C. (2012) 'New lives of teachers' in *Teacher Education Quarterly*, 39(1), pp.7–26.

Dempster, N. and MacBeath, J. (eds.) (2009) *Connecting Leadership and Learning: Principles for Practice*. London: Routledge.

Dempster, N. (2009a) 'What do we know about leadership?' in MacBeath, J. and Dempster, N. (eds.) *Connecting Leadership and Learning*. London: Routledge, pp.20–31.

Dickens, C. (1843) *A Christmas Carol*. London: Chapman & Hall.

DiSC® assessment [online] Available at: www.discprofile.com (Accessed 24 January 2026).

Drucker, P. quoted in David Campbell, David Edgar and George Stonehouse (2011) *Business Strategy: An Introduction* (3rd edn), p.263. London: Palgrave Macmillan.

Durant, W. (1926) *The Story of Philosophy*. New York: Simon & Schuster.

Dweck, C.S. (2012) *Mindset: How You Can Fulfil Your Potential*. London: Robinson.

Erikson, T. (2025) *Surrounded by Idiots: The Four Types of Human Behaviour and How to Effectively Communicate with Each in Business (and in Life)*. New York: Macmillan.

Esquith, R. (2007) *Teach Like Your Hair's on Fire*. London: Penguin Books.

Fullan, M. (2003) *The Moral Imperative of School Leadership*. Thousand Oaks, CA: Corwin Press.

Fullan, M. (2003a) 'Changing the Context' in *The Moral Imperative of School Leadership*. London: Sage.

Fullan, M. (2003b) *Change Forces with a Vengeance*. New York: RoutledgeFalmer.

Garrett, V. (2005) 'Leading and Managing Change' in Davies, B., Ellison, L. and Bowring-Carr, C. (eds.) *School Leadership in the 21st Century: Developing a Strategic Approach*. London: RoutledgeFalmer, pp.72–92.

Gladiator. 2000. [Film]. Ridley Scott. dir. USA: DreamWorks.

Gladwell, M. (2000) *The Tipping Point: How Little Things Can Make a Big Difference*. Boston: Little, Brown and Company.

Goleman, D., Boyatzis, R.E. and McKee, A. (2002) *Primal Leadership: Realizing the Power of Emotional Intelligence*. Boston: Harvard Business School Press.

Gruenert, S. and Whitaker, T. (2017) *School Culture Rewired: How to Define, Assess, and Transform It*. Bloomington, IN: Solution Tree Press.

Hargreaves, A. (1992) 'Foreword' in Hargreaves, A. and Fullan, M. (eds) *Understanding Teacher Development*. London: Cassell.

Hargreaves, A. (2009) 'The Fourth Way of Change: Towards an Age of Inspiration and Sustainability' in Hargreaves, A. and Fullan, M. (eds) *Change Wars*. Bloomington, IN: Solution Tree, pp.11–44.

Hargreaves, A. and Fullan, M. (2012) 'Investing in Capability and Commitment' in *Professional Capital: Transforming Teaching in Every School*. Abingdon: Routledge, pp.46–77.

Hargreaves, A. and Fullan, M. (2012a) *Professional Capital: Transforming Teaching in Every School*. New York: Teachers College Press.

Harris, A. (2008) *Distributed School Leadership: Developing Tomorrow's Leaders*. Abingdon: Routledge.

Henry, T. (2013) *Die Empty: Unleash Your Best Work Every Day*. New York: Portfolio.

Honda Accord® (2003) *Cog* [Advertisement on ITV Television]. 6 April 2003.

Hurley, C. (ed.) (2002) *Could Do Better*. London: Simon & Schuster, quoted in 'Revealing celebrity school reports' (2002) *BBC News* [online] Available at: http://news.bbc.co.uk/1/hi/education/2481573.stm (Accessed: 27 January 2026).

Inception. 2010. [Film]. Christopher Nolan. dir. USA: Warner Bros.

Insights Discovery® colours tool [online] Available at: www.insights.com/products/insights-discovery (Accessed: 24 January 2026).

Karate Kid. 1984. [Film]. John G. Avildsen. dir. USA: Columbia Pictures.

Keating, L.A. and Heslin, P.A. (2015). 'The potential role of mindsets in unleashing employee engagement' in *Human Resource Management Review,* 25(4), 329–341 [online] Available at: https://doi.org/10.1016/j.hrmr.2015.01.008

Krogerus, M. and Tschäppeler, R. (2007) *The Decision Book: Fifty Models for Strategic Thinking.* London: Profile Books.

Leithwood, K. and Day, C. (eds.) (2006) *Seven Strong Claims about Successful Leadership.* London: DfES.

Lingard, B., Hays, D., Mills, M. and Christie, P. (2003) 'Leading Theory' in *Leading Learning: Making Hope Practical in Schools.* Maidenhead: Open University Press, pp.51–78.

Loehr, J. and Schwartz, T. (2003) *The Power of Full Engagement: Managing Energy, Not Time, Is the Key to High Performance and Personal Renewal.* New York: Simon & Schuster.

Myers-Briggs Type Indicator® [online] Available at: www.themyersbriggs.com (Accessed: 24 January 2026).

Nike (1997) *Failure* [Advertisement on YouTube].

Orwell, G. (1945) *Animal Farm.* London: Secker & Warburg.

Portnoy, G. (1983) 'Cheers Theme' from *Theme from Cheers.* Los Angeles, CA: Paramount.

Priestley, M. (2015) 'Teacher agency: What is it and why does it matter?' in *BERA Blog,* British Educational Research Association.

Radcliffe, S. (2009) *Leadership: Plain and Simple.* Harlow: Pearson/Financial Times Publishing.

Rose, J. and Medway, F.J. (1981) 'Measurement of teachers' beliefs in their control over student outcome' in *Journal of Educational Research,* 74, pp.185–190.

Rotter, J.B. (1966) 'Generalized expectancies for internal versus external control of reinforcement' in *Psychological Monographs: General and Applied,* 80(1), pp.1–28.

Schön, D. (1995) 'The new scholarship requires a new epistemology', *Change,* 27(6), pp.26–34.

Senge, P.M. (2006) *The Fifth Discipline: The Art and Practice of the Learning Organization.* London: Random House Business (Revised edition).

Sinek, S. (2009) *Start With Why.* London: Portfolio.

Syed, M. (2016) *Black Box Thinking.* London: John Murray.

The Pursuit of Happyness. 2006. [Film]. Gabriele Muccino. dir. USA: Columbia Pictures.